# PIRATES & PRIVATEERS IN MAURITIUS

DENIS PIAT

Apart from the documents mentioned below, all illustrations in this book are from the collection of Denis Piat, who did the high-resolution photography and provided the captions for them.

The author would like to thank all those who granted permissions in the reproduction of their documents and images: Colonel Hugh Woodes Rogers, OBE: 13; The Library of Congress, Washington, DC: 14, 26, 49; Christian le Comte: 52, 58, 80 (Willoughby), 89; Gérard Gémin: 32–33; L'Echoppe Marine, Village Suisse, Paris: 35, 53; Patrick Ferrat: 60 (treasure map); Collection Denis Piat: 65 (doubloon), 84 (sabre briquet and boarding cutlass), 118 (Chinese compass), 119 (n° 2, 3 and 4: porcelain from the *Geunieerde Provincien*), 122 (piastres and musket balls from the *Saint-Géran*), 126, 130 (octant), 142; National History Museum, Mahébourg: 83, 90 (Drieu's and Rivington's cutlasses), 108, 117 (astrolabe from the *Banda*), 119 (n° 1: porcelain from the *Banda*), 121 (coins from the wreck of the *Speaker*), 122 (thimble from the *Saint-Géran*), 123 (ship's bell from the *Saint-Géran*); Maryse Piat Collection: 84 (the frigate *Chiffone*), 127 (*HMS Magicienne*), 139; Mauritius Commercial Bank Collection: 94–95; Julie de Gersigny: 101; private collection: 112, 123 (spoon from the *Saint-Géran*), 128.

The author would also like to thank François Lamusse for so skilfully showing him the isolated places and hard-to-access places where one can find the rock engravings of the Barachois de Belmont. He would also like to express his sincere gratitude to Christian le Comte who published an earlier edition of this work, and who gave permission for the reproduction of his photographs.

The author would also like to thank Patrick Ferrat, without whom the chapter 'Arrivals, Departures and Sales of Corsairs at Port Louis (1797–1810)' could not have been published.

Finally, the author would like to thank the curator of the Mauritius National History Museum in Mahébourg for kindly authorising the reproduction of several images of objects from the museum.

PHOTO CREDITS:

Natasha de Gersigny-Hein: 13; Christian le Comte: 28, 29, 80 (Willoughby), 83, 89, 90, 108, 121, 122 (thimble from the *Saint-Géran*), 123 (spoon from the *Saint-Géran*); Denis Piat: 35, 37, 53, 60 (treasure map), 65, 70, 84 (cutlasses and the frigate *Chiffone*), 101 (Decaen's signature), 112, 115 (Surcouf Street in Pondichéry), 116 (aerial view), 118, 119, 122, (piastres and musket balls from the *Saint-Géran*), 126, 127, 128, 130, 139, 142; Mauritius Museum Council: 117 (astrolabe); Historic Marine, Goodlands: 124 (model of the *Saint-Géran*); Yann von Arnim: 129.


Originally published in French by Les Éditions du Pacifique in 2014.
Text translation by: Philippa Richmond
Editors: Valerie Ho, Ong Sze Yoong
Editorial Director: Douglas Amrine
Designers: Sandrine Duvillier, Pascal Chan
Production Manager: Sin Kam Cheong
Printed in Singapore by Tian Wah Press
ISBN: 978-981-4385-66-4

FRONT COVER: An *Ara macao*, or scarlet macaw, that pirates often carried on their shoulders; a 19th-century French man-of-war during a naval battle.

BACK COVER: Captain Robert Surcouf aboard the *Hasard*, preparing his crew to board the *Triton* in the Bay of Bengal in 1796.

PAGE 4: Map of Madagascar from Alain Manesson Mallet's Description de l'Univers, published in 1683, two years before the first pirates settled in the bays of the main island and on Île Sainte Marie. The position and names of the neighbouring islands may be somewhat confusing for the contemporary reader.

PAGES 6 & 7: Barbarossa being officially received by Suleiman the Magnificent at Constantinople on 16 May 1534.
*Drawing by C. Ciappori, engraved by Follet for D.Cavaillès Editeur, 19th century.*

# PIRATES & PRIVATEERS IN MAURITIUS

DENIS PIAT

edm EDITIONS DIDIER MILLET

Septentrion
Isle de Madagascar dite de St Laurens ou Isle Daufine
C.Natal
C.St Sebastian
Aro
le Cap Rond
Soarez
Montangnes de Vingagora
Vohemaro
C. de Cocoru
Cap St Andre
St Angelo
OCEAN
Port de St Andre
C.St Antoine
Canha
Antsianach
I.Sta Maria
Bans de Sable
Terre de St Andre
Manangourou R.
Arco
MERI
Pracel
Pays
C de Bout
Desert
I.Ste Apolline
Mansiatre R.
Port aux Prunes
DIONAL
Port de Nansio
Incognu
Terre Rouge
de Bohitsmene
Antavares
Guda
I.Maitre
Port de St Vincent
S.Vincent
Cohaa
Matane
I de Mascaregni ou de Bourbon
Ranoumerca R.
Manarari
Pays des Lafe
Camba
Baye St Andre
Onglahe
Renauoure
Pays des Pierres
Fort des Francois ou des Gallions
Machiores
Tropique de Capricorne
Fort des Bretons
Manampani R.
Fangatores
Vallee d'Ambou
Ste Luce
le Porte de Tonnerre
Carcanossi
Fort Dauphin
Manabauer R.
Ampatres
Fanstere
Cap St Sebastien
Occident
Orient
Midy
65
70
75
10
15
20

# CONTENTS

INTRODUCTION 9

THE PIRATES IN THE INDIAN OCEAN 13

- Henry Every (1653–1728)
- John Bowen (1660–1705)
- Life with the Brethren of the Coast in Madagascar
- Christopher Condent (?–1734)
- Edward England (?–1720)
- Olivier Le Vasseur (1680–1730)
- Other Indian Ocean Pirates
- The Descendants of the Pirates and Queen Bety
- Treasure Hunting in Mauritius

PRIVATEERS IN THE INDIAN OCEAN 75

- François Yves Carosin (1762–1794)
- François Thomas Le Même (1764–1805)
- Joachim Marie Drieu (1767–1835)
- Jacques François Perroud (1770–1822)
- Jean Marie Dutertre (1770–1811)
- Robert Surcouf (1773–1827)
- Other Privateers in the Indian Ocean

SHIPWRECKS AROUND MAURITIUS 117

- The *Banda*
- The *Geunieerde Provincien*
- The *Speaker*
- The *Saint-Géran*
- HMS *Sirius*
- HMS *Magicienne*
- The *Coureur*
- Other Wrecks

ARRIVALS, DEPARTURES AND SALE OF PRIVATEER VESSELS IN PORT LOUIS (1797–1810) 135

BIBLIOGRAPHY 141

# INTRODUCTION

It is believed that Dutch pirates were the first to frequent the warm seas of the Indian Ocean and establish bases in Madagascar. During the 1630s, they started attacking the convoys of the VOC (Vereenigde Oost-Indische Compagnie – the Dutch East India Company). These convoys came from Bantam (now Banten in northwest Java) or Manila loaded with spices, silver and fine porcelain from China, and would often stop over at Madagascar before heading for the Cape of Good Hope en route to Amsterdam or Rotterdam. The English ships of the East India Company also aroused the interest of the Dutch pirates, but the Royal Navy succeeded in discouraging and eliminating them from the region thanks to its tenacity and firepower.

By the end of the 17th century, English and Spanish naval forces had harassed the numerous English and American pirates present in the Caribbean to the point where, feeling seriously threatened, they had begun a gradual shift to the Indian Ocean. The pirates first appeared there around 1685, settling in bays and coves on the northeastern shores of the island of Madagascar.

Pursued by the English and French navies, the pirate numbers started to drop from 1718 and, from around 1730, the Indian Ocean was considered to be almost entirely free from this blight. For the following half century, the seas of the region were reasonably secure, except during the years 1756 to 1763.

OPPOSITE: The coconut palm, the tree of the islands, first discovered by sailors in the 18th century.
*Engraving by E.Guérin, Paris, 19th century.*

In 1778, war broke out between England and France, but the French Navy had been weakened by the upheavals of the Revolution back home. The government, therefore, decided to encourage individuals and private shipowners to take up privateering, as was permitted by the maritime laws of the period. Thus, from 1780, soon after the beginning of the American War of Independence, the first French privateers began to set up business in the Indian Ocean, fortified by their status as official auxiliary combatants.

These privateers wasted no time in establishing their base on Île de France (present-day Mauritius), and soon over a hundred of them were harassing the East India Company's convoys. Their repeated attacks on and captures of English merchantmen (trading ships) grew to the point that the British authorities decided that they had to put an end to this "nest of privateers" that was doing so much damage to Britain's economy and power. The English assembled all their maritime forces in the region and successively captured the islands of Rodrigues and Bonaparte (present-day Réunion, which was restored to France with the Treaty of Paris in 1815). Then, on 2 December 1810, the English unleashed large numbers of well-armed troops on the north of Île de France. The French regiment there put up a stubborn defence, but their efforts were in vain.

Overwhelmed, the last French governor, General Decaen, signed an "honourable capitulation" on 3 December 1810. The island was turned over to the British and the war against the privateers was over.

OPPOSITE: (Detail) The HCS *Sir David Scott* was an East Indiaman belonging to the English East India Company. Even though these vessels were well armed, they were still coveted by French corsairs. *Engraving by William J. Huggins, 1830.*

### A few designations and abbreviations of the British Navy:

East Indiaman: normally refers to a vessel, armed or otherwise, under charter or license to the English East India Company. In this book the term shall be used to refer to vessels sailing for any of the East India companies.
HCS: Honourable Company's Ship. Prefix for ships of the English East India Company.
HMS: Her/His Majesty's Ship. Prefix for Royal Navy ships.

BARBEROUSSE.

## THE PIRATES OF THE INDIAN OCEAN

The word 'pirate' comes from the Greek *peirates*, the name given to the brigands against whom Pompey launched an expedition in Greece and Asia Minor in 67 BC. By extension, contemporary pirates are bandits who scour the seas, attacking and plundering vessels which cross their paths, with the further distinction that they operate in times of both peace and war.

Supported by the Ottoman Empire, piracy flourished in the Mediterranean during the 15th century, reaching its peak during the 16th century with the dominance of the Barbary corsairs. In effect, Berber piracy was a form of warfare against the European states. In 1516, the infamous Barbarossa brothers, Aruj and Hayreddin, transformed the town of Algiers into a Mediterranean stronghold from which, with the support of Suleiman the Magnificent, they led expeditions against the Holy Roman Empire ruled by Charles V. These incessant attacks on European ships continued right up to 1830 when Algiers was finally taken by a squadron led by the French Admiral Victor-Guy Duperré, former captain of the *Bellone* and squadron commander at the naval battle of Grand Port in 1810.

Piracy in the Indian Ocean, however, traces its roots back to the West Indies and the Caribbean Sea. After Christopher Columbus' arrival on the island of Hispaniola (sometimes called Santo Domingo – now split between Haiti and the Dominican Republic) in 1492, Spanish navigators, explorers

ABOVE: (Detail) Captain Woodes Rogers (circa 1679–1732), navigator, privateer, and Royal Governor of the Bahamas. He eradicated piracy from the Caribbean. His motto was: "While I breathe, I hope".
*Painting by William Hogarth, circa 1729.*

OPPOSITE: Portrait of Hayreddin, better known as Barbarossa. He was born at Mytilene on Lesbos, circa 1476. He died on 4 July 1546 in Constantinople. Along with the Genoese admiral Andrea Doria, he was one of the greatest seamen of his time.
*Engraved by Maurin, Paris, 1836.*

and adventurers frequented the territories of South America, stripping the Amerindian civilisations of their riches. During the 16th century, the Spanish transported the equivalent of three times Europe's total stock of gold and silver from the New World back to Spain. The Caribbean islands were ideal ports of call for their returning ships. The precious cargo aboard these ships soon attracted attention and it was not long before the first Caribbean pirates appeared. Convoy stragglers and ships separated from their convoys by bad weather became the objects of systematic attacks. The island of Saint Martin, uninhabited until 1617, offered the pirates an ideal lair. Subsequently, Île à Vache, south of Haiti, and then, from 1630, Île de la Tortue (Tortuga), to the north of Haiti, became the pirates' main haunt.

From 1648, the development of a French colony on the island of Saint Barthélemy enabled the Spanish galleons to use it as a refurbishment base on the West Indies route – a situation which did not go unnoticed by the pirates. Attacks against these rich convoys increased and their success contributed significantly to the development of piracy in the region.

ABOVE: Some pirate captains wore refined and luxurious clothes in imitation of the English nobility. Captain Bartholomew Roberts (1682–1722), known as Black Bart, was an English buccaneer-turned-pirate whose real name was John Roberts. He was one of the most notorious pirates of his time. *Engraving, 1725.*

OPPOSITE: Turgut Reis, also known as Dragut (circa 1520–1565). A Turkish disciple of Barbarossa, he was a bloodthirsty pirate operating in the Mediterranean before becoming a corsair, and then an admiral of the Ottoman Empire. He defeated the Spanish at the naval battle of Djerba in 1560. *Engraving taken from* Histoire des Pirates, *D.Cavaillès éditeur, 1846.*

## Periods of piracy in the Caribbean

**1521–1561:** Preponderantly French, the highlight of this period was the capture, by Jean Fleury and Jean Ango in 1523, of a Spanish galleon carrying 58,000 gold ingots along with Moctezuma's ransom. The fabulous booty was taken back to Dieppe.

**1562–1621:** Domination of the English Sea Dogs under Elizabeth I. Their ranks included Sir John Hawkins, Sir Francis Drake and Sir Walter Raleigh.

**1622–1655:** Predominance of Dutch pirates and buccaneers such as Jan Hendricksz, Willem Schouten and Piet Heyn.

**1656–1671:** The capture of Jamaica and Port Royal in 1655 by Sir William Penn and Robert Venables set off the golden age of freebooters and buccaneers. Attacks on Spanish ports were launched from Jamaica and Haiti. Panama was taken by Sir Henry Morgan in 1671.

**1672–1722:** Decline followed by the demise of the pirates, who were hounded to oblivion by English (Woodes Rogers and William Dampier), French and Spanish squadrons.

A. DEDELLE, DEL.

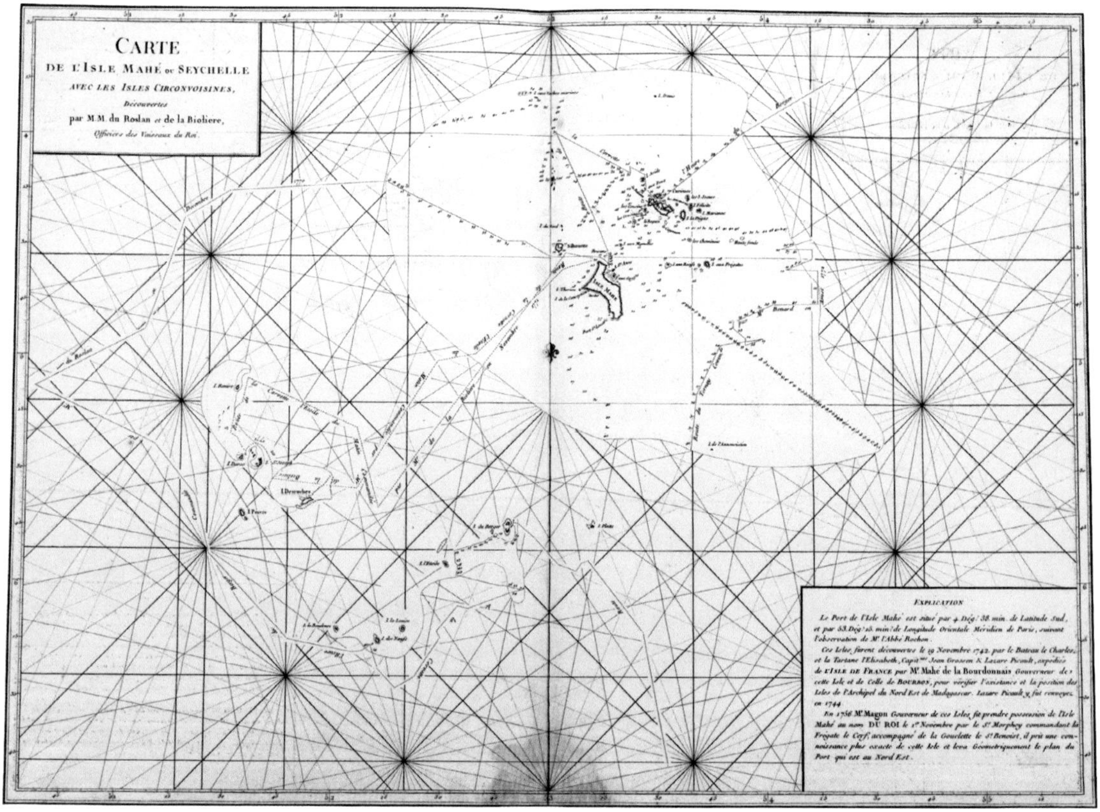


18th-century map of Mahé and neighbouring islands in the Seychelles. Under the orders of Bertrand-François Mahé de La Bourdonnais, Captains Lazare Picault and Jean Grossen took possession of the island on 19 November 1742 and named it Mahé. Silhouette Island, also in the Seychelles, was probably a long-time pirate den.

Some pirates, such as Nau (known as the Olonnais, as he came from the Sables-d'Olonne in France) and Henry Morgan, were known for their cruelty and much-feared in the area. Another bloodthirsty pirate was Montbars the Exterminator, who distinguished himself through his cruelty, cunning and number of prizes, and served as the inspiration for both Captain Hook and Red Rackham. Mary Read and Anne Bonny were no less reputed for their aggressiveness and sowed terror throughout the Caribbean. Edward Teach, known as Blackbeard, was probably one of the last pirates in the region.

Pirate bases were established on the island of Providence (now New Providence) in the Bahamas, then on Guinea and Sierra Leone, from which the freebooters were able to enter the slave trade, supplying New York, Charleston, and Virginia with slaves, gold and ivory, which they obtained along the African coast. In his book *Sous le Pavillon Noir, Pirates et Flibustiers*, Philippe Jacquin claims that for several decades during this period there were approximately five thousand pirates in operation at any time, three-quarters of whom were English or American.

Throughout the 17th century, however, the colonies and national navies developed and grew stronger. Beginning in 1680, the Spanish established a series of naval bases, at Veracruz in Mexico, Portobello in Panama and Cartagena in Columbia – as did the English in Jamaica – from which the pirates were relentlessly hunted down.

From 1685, therefore, the pirates gradually abandoned the Caribbean in favour of the Indian Ocean. English and American pirates, such as John Bowen, Henry Every, William Kidd and Thomas Tew, set up base in the bays of northern Madagascar, between Tamatave and the Bay of Antongil, and particularly on Île Sainte Marie[1] in the district of Nosy Boraha. French pirates, such as Olivier Le Vasseur, also known as La Bouche or La Buse (the buzzard), and Olivier Misson, soon followed.

In 1690, influenced by Misson, who was a Huguenot, and Angelo Caracioli, a defrocked Dominican priest and fellow pirate, there may have been an attempt to create a pirate utopia, called Libertalia, to the north of the Bay of Diego Suarez. To this day, however, opinion on the issue continues to be divided, and piracy experts have yet to confirm the veracity of this story.

Ali Kodja (?–1818) was a Mediterranean pirate who was feared for his cruelty. He was appointed Dey of Algiers in 1817, upon which, fearing for his safety, he gave orders for 1,500 janissaries to be executed. These elite soldiers had plotted the assassination of his predecessor, Omar Agha. Kodja died of the plague in 1818, after only a few months in power.
*Engraving taken from Histoires des Pirates, D.Cavaillès éditeur, 1846.*

**PAGES 18 & 19:** Mausoleums of the kings of Golconda (Deccan, eastern India).
*Copper engraving by Léonce Lhuillier, Imprimerie Legay, Paris, 1830.*

1. Before being named Santa Maria by the Portuguese in the 16th century, Île Sainte Marie was known under the names Anosiborahy, Nosy Boraha or Nosy Ibrahim (island of Ibrahim). Île Sainte Marie is 8 miles from the main island of Madagascar, 37 miles long and 4 miles wide.

Several other English pirates also settled in the area and set about terrorising commercial shipping. The Comoros, the Mascarenes, and the Seychelles all provided more-or-less permanent bases for pirates, in a period when attempts by the French to establish a colonial foothold in Madagascar and Île Bourbon (present-day Réunion) and similar ventures by the Dutch in Mauritius were still in their infancy, and there were no military bases capable of ensuring safe passage in the region. The pirates, therefore, had free rein to conduct their daring attacks against Portuguese, Dutch, English and French shipping. Flying the Jolly Roger, the infamous skull and crossbones flag, they would sail towards the Malabar Coast, the Red Sea, and the Persian Gulf, where they harassed and plundered ships carrying the legendary riches of Indian Princes and the Arabs of Oman. Laden with spices, precious cloths, and slaves, the numerous trading ships in the region served as attractive targets.

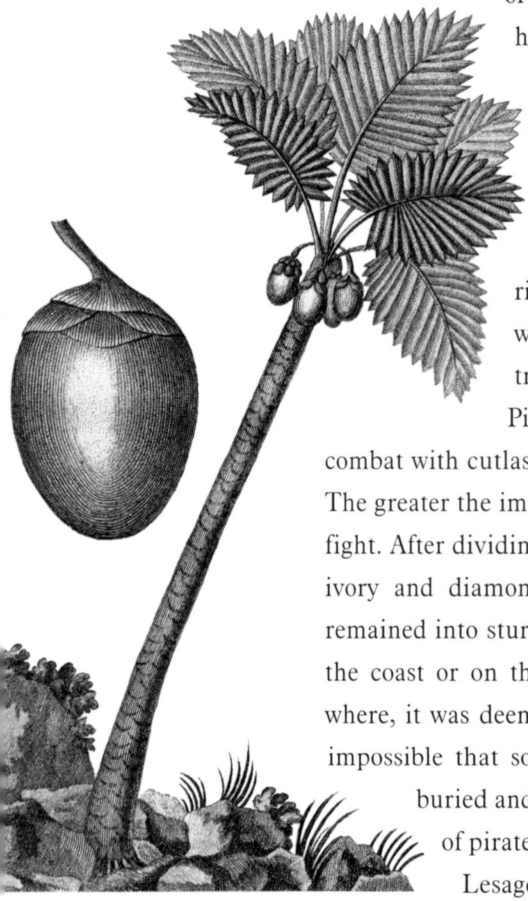

Pirate attacks were often fierce, and involved close combat with cutlasses, marlinspikes, pistols, muskets, axes and grenades. The greater the imagined worth of the booty, the harder the pirates would fight. After dividing the spoils of pearls, precious stones, silverware, gold, ivory and diamonds among the crew, the captain would place what remained into sturdy sea chests. These were then buried or hidden along the coast or on the deserted islands of the Indian Ocean archipelagos where, it was deemed, they would be safer than on board ship. It is not impossible that some of these treasure chests are still in these places, buried and waiting. After all, other tangible traces of the presence of pirates have been found. For instance, on the beaches of Anse Lesage and at Grand'Anse on Frégate Island in the Seychelles, there are a large teak mast, the ruins of a forge, and three graves on which sabre handles had once been placed.

In 1695, a number of pirates abandoned their marauding ways and settled on Île Bourbon. Captain Henry Every off-loaded dozens of freebooters onto the island. Around fifty of them were granted amnesties; they were assimilated into the island's population and became peaceful settlers. Twenty or so tried to escape, and were taken prisoner by the squadron of Captain de Serquigny, who returned them to France. Several other pirates, such as Howell Davis, Edward England, John Taylor and Olivier Le Vasseur, frequently visited Île Bourbon. Captain Thomas White unloaded some of his freebooters there during a sojourn at Saint-Paul. Captain Christopher Condent and his 135 crewmen were granted amnesties and settled on the island. After a final trip to Mauritius, then occupied by the Dutch, John Bowen settled in Bourbon in 1704. His retirement on the French colony, however, did not last long: he died a few months later, in 1705.

It is estimated that, between 1685 and 1730, there were around 1,000 pirates operating in the Indian Ocean. The determination, however, of the deputy governor of Île Bourbon, Antoine Desforges-Boucher, and that of the English authorities, eventually won out. The Royal Navy squadron commanded by Commodore Thomas Matthews subdued them with amnesties or by force. Pirate activity began to diminish significantly in 1718 and, by 1730, the region was considered free of this "sea scum".

## Henry Every (1653–1728)

One of the most infamous and terrifying of all the English pirates, Henry Every (also known as Henry or John Avery, or Long Ben) was probably born in the Plymouth area in 1653. Born the son of an English grocer, he started his seafaring life as a sailor in the Royal Navy.

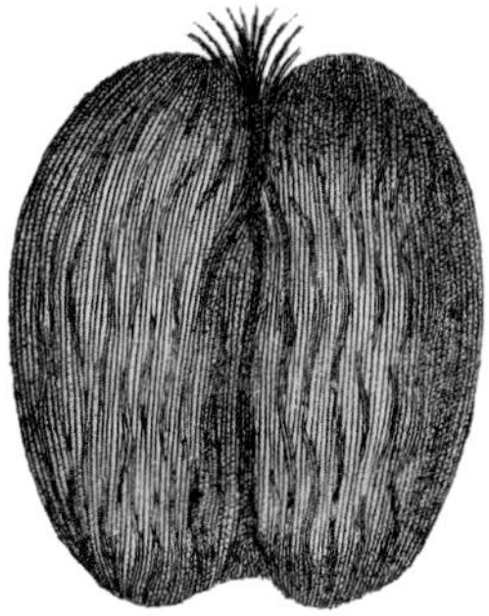

**ABOVE:** A coco de mer nut without its encasing fibrous husk. It is not difficult to see how it acquired a reputation of possessing aphrodisiac qualities.
*Engraving, 18th century.*

**OPPOSITE:** The coco de mer (*Lodoicea maldivica*) was thought to be endemic to the islands of Praslin and Curieuse in the Seychelles. In the past, sailors attributed aphrodisiac qualities to the plant.
*Engraving, 18th century.*

**PAGE 22:** Île de France, now Mauritius.
*Map, 18th century.*

**PAGE 23:** Rodrigues Island.
*Map, 18th century.*

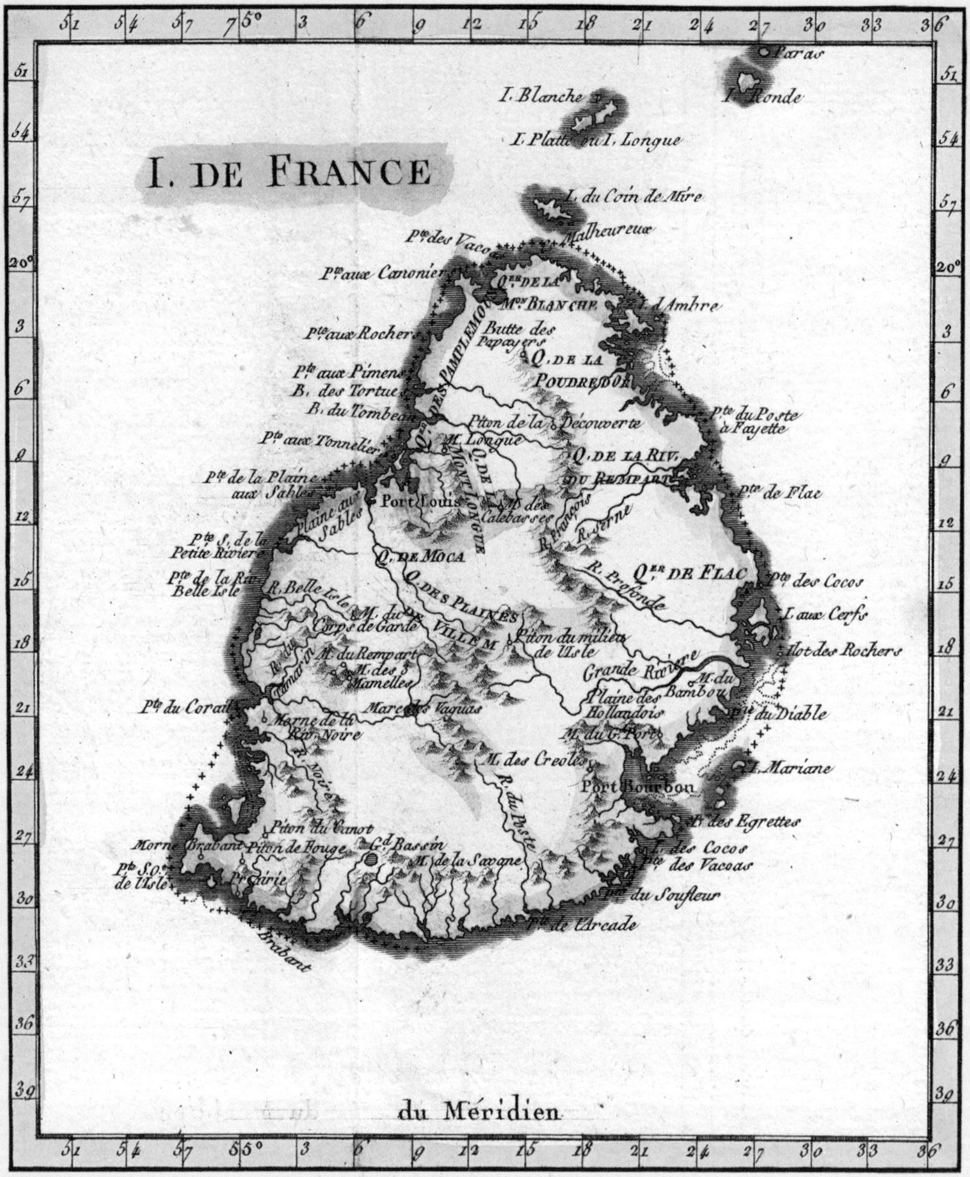
I. DE FRANCE
Paras
I. Ronde
I. Blanche
I. Platte ou I. Longue
I. du Coin de Mire
Malheureux
Pte. aux Canonier
Qer. DE LA
Mn. BLANCHE
I. d'Ambre
Pte. aux Rochers
Butte des Papayers
Q. DE LA POUDRE D'OR
Pte. aux Pimens
B. des Tortue
B. du Tombeau
Piton de la Découverte
Pte. du Poste à Fayette
Pte. aux Tonnelier
M. Longue
Q. DE LA RIV. DU REMPART
Pte. de la Plaine aux Sables
Port Louis
Ms. des Calebasses
Pte. de Flac
Plaine aux Sables
R. François
R. Serne
Pte. S. de la Petite Riviere
Q. DE MOCA
Qer. DE FLAC
R. Profonde
Pte. de la Riv. Belle Isle
Q. DES PLAINES
Pte. des Cocos
I. aux Cerfs
Corps de Garde
Piton du milieu de l'Isle
Ilot des Rochers
M. du Rempart
M. des 3 Mamelles
Grande Riviere
M. du Bambou
Plaine des Hollandois
Pte. du Corail
Mare des Vaquas
Pte. du Diable
Morne de la Riv. Noire
M. du Gd. Port
R. Noire
M. des Creoles
I. Mariane
Port Bourbon
R. du Poste
Piton du Canot
Is. des Egrettes
Morne Brabant
Piton de Rouge
Gd. Bassin
I. des Cocos
M. de la Savane
Pte. des Vacoas
Pte. S.O. de l'Isle
Pte. du Soufleur
Pte. de l'Arcade
Brabant
du Méridien
20°
55°

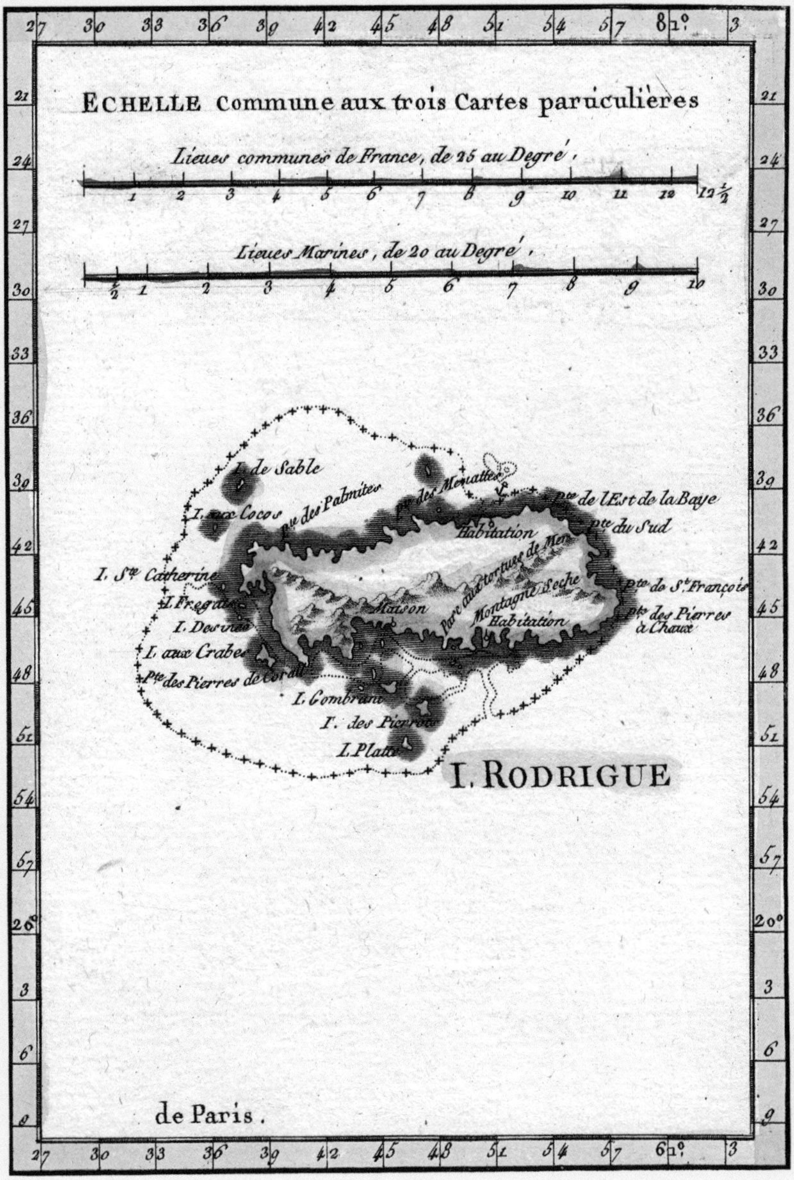
ECHELLE Commune aux trois Cartes particulières
Lieues communes de France, de 25 au Degré.
Lieues Marines, de 20 au Degré.
I. de Sable
I. aux Cocos
Pte des Palmites
Pte des Manattes
Pte de l'Est de la Baye
Pte du Sud
Habitation
I. Ste Catherine
I. Fregate
I. Des ines
I. aux Crabes
Pte des Pierres de Corail
Maison
Parc aux tortues de Mer
Montagne Seche
Habitation
Pte de St. François
Pte des Pierres à Chaux
I. Gombrani
I. des Pierrots
I. Plate
I. RODRIGUE
de Paris.

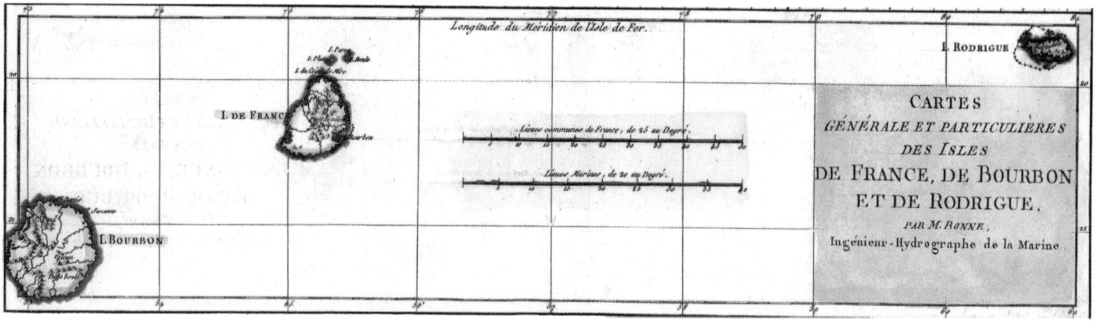


**ABOVE:** Map of the Mascarene Archipelago by Rigobert Bonne, cartographer and hydrographer of the French Navy, 1763.

**BELOW:** Henry Every's flag. The mere sight of it made more than one captain shiver in his boots.

**OPPOSITE:** Île Bourbon, now Réunion Island.
*Map, 18th century.*

Little is known for certain about Every's early career, though many versions of the story exist. The most likely claims that he led a mutiny on board the *Charles*, whose captain was a certain Charles Gibson, and took command of the vessel. He renamed her the *Fancy* and took her on a campaign in the seas around the Cape Verde Islands, off the west coast of Africa, during which he captured three English ships.

Then, while sailing off the coast of Guinea, Every developed a highly lucrative strategy: approaching the shore, the *Fancy* would hoist the English flag. Eager to trade with the English, the locals would hasten aboard the *Fancy*, loaded with plenty of gold in order to do business. Once they were aboard, however, Captain Every and his crew would throw themselves upon them, seizing their gold and reducing the poor souls to slavery. In this way Every became extremely rich.

Every then attacked and captured two Danish vessels, one of which he burned, while the other continued its journey alongside the *Fancy*. Long Ben was now in command of 150 men and 56 cannons. However, things soon began to go wrong on the Danish vessel – probably the threat of mutiny – and Every decided to abandon it.

Subsequently, Every descended the west coast of Africa, passing the Cape of Good Hope before stopping at Île Bourbon in 1687, where he relieved

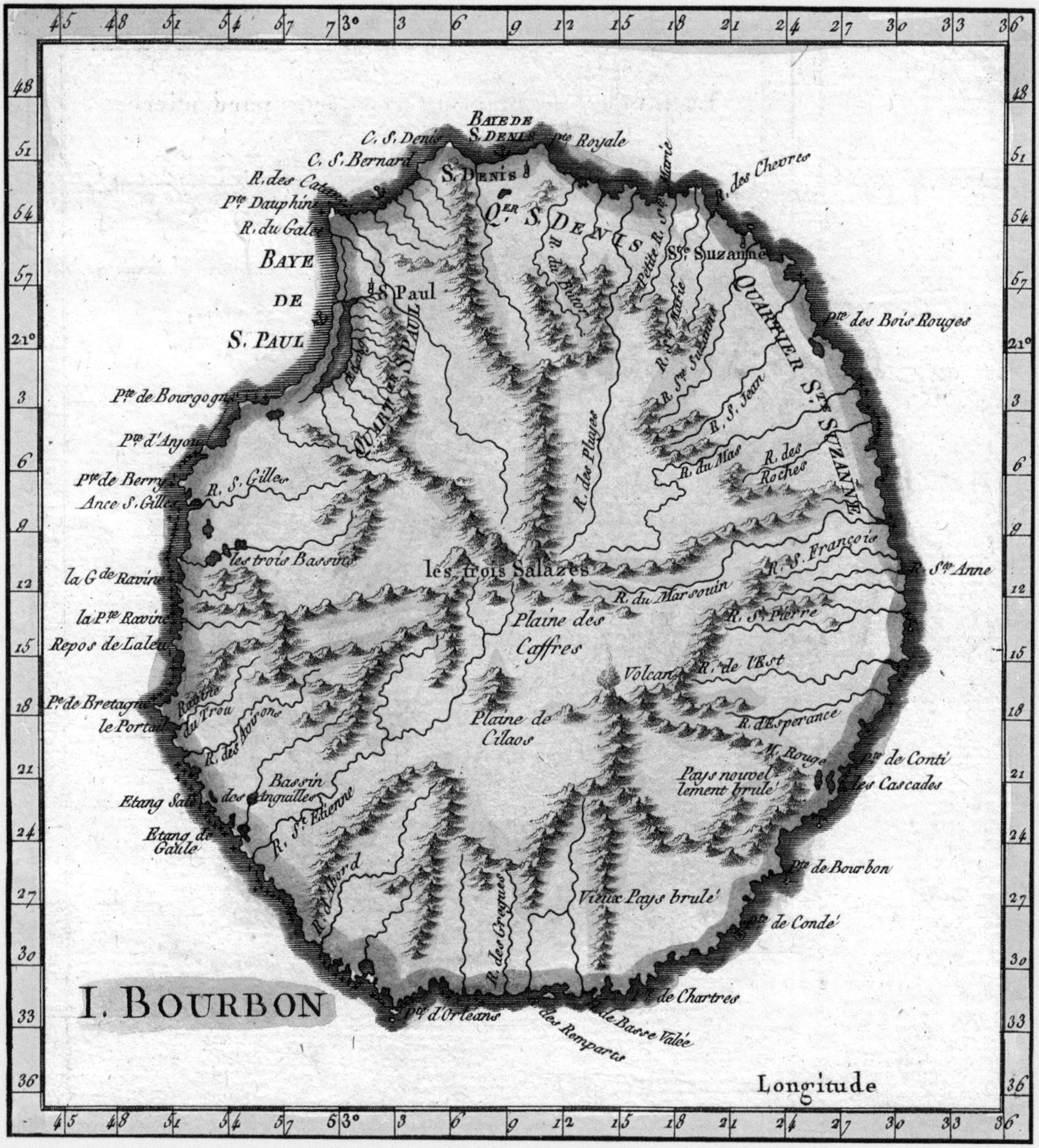

I. BOURBON
BAYE DE S. DENIS
C. S. Denis
Pte Royale
C. S. Bernard
S. Denis
R. des Chevres
Pte Dauphine
R. du Galet
Qer S. Denis
R. du Butor
Petite R. Ste Marie
Ste Suzanne
BAYE DE S. PAUL
S. Paul
Quartier S. Paul
Quartier Ste Suzanne
Pte des Bois Rouges
R. Ste Marie
R. Ste Suzanne
R. S. Jean
Pte de Bourgogne
Pte d'Anjou
R. des Plages
R. du Mas
R. des Roches
Pte de Berry
R. S. Gilles
Ance S. Gilles
les trois Bassins
les trois Salazes
R. S. François
R. Ste Anne
la Gde Ravine
R. du Marsouin
R. S. Pierre
la Pte Ravine
Plaine des Caffres
Repos de Laleu
Volcan
R. de l'Est
Pte de Bretagne
le Portail
Ravine du Trou
R. des Avirons
Plaine de Cilaos
R. d'Esperance
M. Rouge
Pte de Conti
les Cascades
Pays nouvellement brulé
Bassin des Anguilles
Etang Salé
R. St Etienne
Etang de Gaule
Pte de Bourbon
R. d'Abord
Vieux Pays brulé
R. des Gregues
Pte de Condé
de Chartres
Pte d'Orleans
des Remparts
de Basse Valée
Longitude

himself of about 70 extremely wealthy pirates. Amongst them were Jacques Beda, Jean Bloqueman, Jean Selin, Gilbert Wildman and the Dutchman Jan Pieter Sekeling[2], all of whom settled down to a peaceful existence on the island. Captain Every then sailed for Madagascar to rejoin his stooges and to repair and re-provision his boat. He ended up spending several years based at Nosy Mangabe in the Bay of Antongil, where he soon became known as the King of Madagascar.

In June 1695, Captain Every set sail for the Red Sea and the Persian Gulf to prey on ships carrying riches and pilgrims to Mecca. The pirates knew their route well: they would go from Surat in India to Mocha in present day Yemen, and then on to Mecca. Every joined up with some other marauders and, in a coordinated effort, they managed to capture the *Fateh Mohamed*. It is said that the infamous pirate Captain Thomas Tew literally lost his head during the boarding. Nevertheless, large quantities of gold and silver were won in the raid.

A few days later, the *Ganj-i-Sawai*, one of the biggest ships of the Great Mughal Emperor Aurangzeb's fleet appeared. Equipped with 40 guns and captained by Muhammad Ibrahim, it was a formidable opponent for the pirates. Nonetheless, the pirates' rapid manoeuvring and accurate cannonfire caused the Mughal's ship to lose its main mast. In addition, one of the *Ganj-i-Sawai*'s cannons exploded on deck. In the subsequent panic, the pirates boarded and quickly took control of the ship.

The officers and rich traders were tortured to reveal where the Mughal's riches were being hidden on board the *Ganj-i-Sawai*, which turned out to be a veritable Aladdin's cave glittering with a staggering quantity of gold and silver, solid gold jewellery, precious stones, and famous diamonds from the

2. According to Marina Carter in *Pirates of Mauritius* (Pink Pigeon Press, London, 2003), Sekeling's descendants on Réunion today are apparently numerous.

## A short pirate glossary

BARBARY

Barbary, or the Barbary states, was the name given by Europeans to the countries of North Africa – Algeria, Tunisia and Tripolitania – the name being derived from that of the Berber peoples who inhabited these lands. The Barbary corsairs were pirates who wrestled with the Europeans for control of the Mediterranean Sea, following the example given by the Barbarossa brothers, infamous pirates who were also the masters of Algiers in the 16th century.

BUCCANEER

In 1630, European adventurers who had settled on Saint Kitts, in the Caribbean, were driven off by the Spanish, and migrated to the island of Tortuga, to the north of Hispaniola. There, they hunted wild oxen to smoke (*boucaner* in French, from which 'buccaneer' is derived) the meat and treat the hides for trade, having learnt both processes from the Arawaks, the local Amerindians. Once again chased out by the Spanish, they turned to freebooting (*see below*).

PRIVATEER

To acknowledge their official function in times of war, privateers were issued a *letter of marque* which authorised their status as auxiliary belligerents. While only supposed to harass the enemy of the issuing country, privateers often went beyond their remit and 'harassed' merchant shipping as well. It was not until the signing of the Declaration of Paris in 1856 that privateering was abolished, although the USA, Spain and Mexico all refused to sign the agreement. 'Privateer' can refer either to individuals or to their ships.

CORSAIR

The word 'corsair' comes from the Latin *cursus* (course, journey, expedition, and, subsequently, plunder) via *corsaro* in Italian and *corsaire* in French. Effectively a privateer, particularly as applied to Barbary pirates or corsairs (*see above*) and to French privateers and their ships.

FREEBOOTER

From the Dutch *vrijbuit* meaning plunder, hence *vrijbuiter* meaning plunderer. Originally referring to an unpaid privateer operating in the Caribbean, the term has become a general one for anyone doing pirate-like things off his own back.

BRETHREN OF THE COAST

Also called the Brothers or Brotherhood of the Coast. A somewhat egalitarian brotherhood formed by freebooters during the 17th century in the West Indies. For a long time, they scoured the Caribbean Sea, before moving on to the Indian Ocean.

PIRATE

A sea bandit who roams the seas plundering, stealing and pillaging ships for personal profit. If captured, the sentence for a pirate was usually hanging.

ABOVE: Aurangzeb (born 1619), a descendant of Tamerlane, took command of the Mogul Empire in 1659, having imprisoned his father and arranged for the assassination of his three brothers. Despite his religious fanaticism, he was a good administrator and understood the importance of literature and the arts. His reign is viewed as the apogee of the Mogul Empire, although decadence was already beginning to set in before his death in 1707.

*Copper engraving by Bernard Picart, taken from* Histoire Générale de tous les peuples du monde, *Rollin Fils, Paris, 1728.*

OPPOSITE (TOP): Captain Henry Every out on a stroll with his servant.

*Engraving taken from* Histoire des Pirates, *1725.*

OPPOSITE (BOTTOM): Portrait of Captain Every, also known as Long Ben and Captain Bridgeman. Behind him, the *Ganj-i-Sawai*, the jewel of the Great Mogul's fleet, is being boarded.

*Engraving, 1734.*

Kingdom of Golkonda; the haul is estimated to have been worth the equivalent of US$3.3 million today. This prize, taken by Captain Every and his acolytes, was without doubt the largest ever taken during the period of piracy in the Indian Ocean. Each crew member would have had a share equivalent to some US$20,000 at today's rates, in addition to a pile of gems. Furthermore, the *Ganj-i-Sawai* was carrying a Mughal princess who, according to some, Henry Every later married by force.

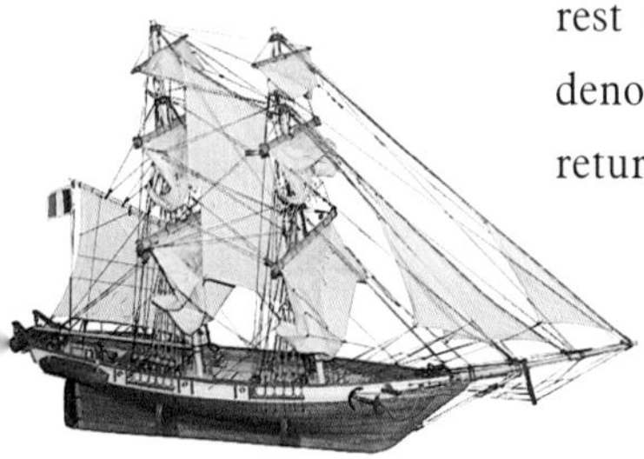

Thereafter, Every sailed off to the Caribbean, probably to the Island of Providence, with his crew and his captured Mogul princess. He spent the rest of his days living under false names, in constant fear of being denounced. Several of his men settled in North America, while others returned to Britain, using pseudonyms to ward off the long arm of the law. For ten of them though, this did not suffice: they were arrested and hanged in 1696.

## John Bowen (1660–1705)

John Bowen was born somewhere in Bermuda in 1660; the exact location remains unknown. Having started his career in the Caribbean, Bowen turned up in the Indian Ocean when he was in his forties.

Bowen was the captain of a ship in the West Indies that was captured by French pirates, whom he then joined on a campaign along the east coast of Africa until they were shipwrecked on Madagascar. Bowen and two of his companions, Thomas White and a certain Boreman, managed to escape and took refuge in the Bay of Saint Augustin in the southwest of Madagascar.

Bowen was then taken on board a ship which went marauding in the company of another ship captained by the pirate George Booth. On 16 April 1701, they encountered the *Speaker*, a superb 450-tonner English slaver (a

ABOVE: A frigate was a three-masted ship which sailed well and was easy to manoeuvre. Being relatively light and fast for its size, it was very effective for pursuing merchant vessels.

*Model made by Comajora, Curepipe, Mauritius.*

OPPOSITE (FROM TOP TO BOTTOM): An 18th-century English merchantman, a typical pirate prey.

*Model made by Historic Marine, Goodlands, Mauritius.*

A brig was a two-masted ship that typically weighed less than 300 tons. It had a large sail area for its size, giving it considerable speed and manoeuvrability, which explains its popularity as a slave ship.

*Model made by Historic Marine, Goodlands, Mauritius.*

A lugger was a small boat, sometimes clinker built, generally with three masts slightly inclined toward the stern. Usually used for transport or fishing, it could also be armed in times of war or for use by corsairs.

*Model made by Historic Marine, Goodlands, Mauritius.*

slave ship) replete with 50 cannons that turned out to be a former French man-of-war (a warship). While the *Speaker* only had a crew of 40 or so men, the combined pirate strength was close to 200 men, and included in its ranks the notorious pirates Thomas Collins and Thomas Howard. Booth, assisted by Bowen and Nathaniel North, directed the attack and it was not long before the *Speaker*'s commander, Captain Eastlake, had surrendered. A certificate to the effect that the ship had been forcibly taken from him, signed by George Booth, John Appowen (John Bowen), and Cornelius George, was made over to Eastlake.

The pirate flotilla then made for Zanzibar, where Booth, having gone ashore to buy provisions, was killed in a brawl with some Arabs. Bowen was elected by the crew to take over as captain of the *Speaker* and they sailed off to hunt along the west coast of India. They managed to take two Arab ships coming out of Surat, and then, on 28 October 1701, they attacked the *Borneo*, an English merchant vessel commanded by Captain Conway. One

of the pirates' prisoners, Thomas Towsey, forced to work as a shipwright (ship's carpenter) on the *Speaker*, later claimed that Bowen, having stripped everything that he wanted from the *Borneo*, sold it to some Indian merchants in Kollam.

A month later, John Bowen gave chase to another English ship, the *Nathaniel*, which he captured with ease. At the beginning of the following year, 1702, a violent cyclone struck the *Speaker* in the vicinity of the Mascarenes. On 7 January, the ship was in great difficulty off the southeast coast of Mauritius, and there was nothing Captain Bowen could do to save it from the wild seas. The *Speaker* crashed into the reefs at the mouth of the Grande Rivière Sud Est, close to the Îlot des Roches. The 170 pirates who were on board, along with the 30 Arab and 12 English prisoners, hastily built rafts, and all made it to land with their weapons. They made camp close to the shore and slaughtered three oxen for dinner. The Dutch governor of the island, Roelof Diodati[3], was soon made aware of their arrival but, having only 52 men at his disposal, he realised that open confrontation with the pirates was disadvantageous. He therefore gave his permission for the injured to be treated and cared for, and for the settlers to sell provisions to the shipwrecked men and treat them "as friends". The pirates spent most of their time going back and forth from the wreck in a couple of small rowing boats, salvaging what they could from it.

A tense atmosphere, however, was ever-present, with each camp fomenting plans to gain control over the other. Eventually, the governor and his council, wishing to put an end to an unsustainable situation, decided to sell Bowen the *Vliegente Hart*, a three-masted schooner. Bowen made a request, which was accepted, for some extra wood to lengthen the boat by four metres. In return, the pirates gave the wreck of the *Speaker* and all that it might still contain to the governor and his council. Captain Bowen and his men finally weighed anchor on 24 March 1702 after nearly three months on Mauritius. They left behind the 30 Arab prisoners taken during the engagements off Surat and the 12 English prisoners taken off the coast of India. The latter were taken aboard some English ships calling at Mauritius the following September.

Having left Mauritius, Bowen and his band of rogues sailed for Île Bourbon where, on 2 April 1702, they took a small Portuguese vessel before continuing on to Madagascar, settling in Matatanes.

Some while later, two Scottish slavers dropped anchor in the bay across from Bowen's camp: the *Speedy Return*, under Captain Robert Drummond, and a brigantine under Captain Stewart named the *Content*. Both vessels were laden with beer, flour, tobacco, moulds for musket balls, ivory-handled

3. Roelof Diodati, Italian by birth, was governor of Mauritius from 1692 to 1703.

OPPOSITE: The governor's residence at Saint Denis on Réunion.
*Engraving drawn by Bulluria, engraved by Couché and Chanain,* France Pittoresque, *19th century.*

PAGES 32 & 33: The Caribbean Sea abounds with islands large and small which, in the 17th century, made ideal hideaways for close to 5,000 pirates of mainly English or American origin. Île à Vache, to the south of Santo Domingo or Hispaniola, and Tortuga to the north served as more permanent pirate bases.
*Map, 18th century.*

CARTE DE L'ISLE DE
SAINT DOMINGUE,
Pour servir a l'Histoire Générale des Voyages.
Par M.B. Ing de la Marine.
Echelle de Lieues comunes de France.
5 10 15 20 25
I. de la T
Cap S. Nicolas
Mole S. Nicolas
Cap aux Foux
la Plateforme
Baye des Gonaives
B. de S Marc
I. DE LA GONAVE
Arcadins
Cap Rose
les Caymites
Baye des Baradaires
C Dame Marie
Nipes
le Rochelois
Miragoane
Petit Goave
l'Acul
Cavaillon
Pointe des Trois
Cap Tiberon
le Fond
Yaquin
les Anglois
Port à Piment
S. Louis
Yaquin
Cap Benet
Pointe à Gravois
I. A VACHE
Pointe de l'Abacou
Longitude Occidentale du Méridien de
21
30
20
30m
19
30
18
30
17
77
30
76
30m
75

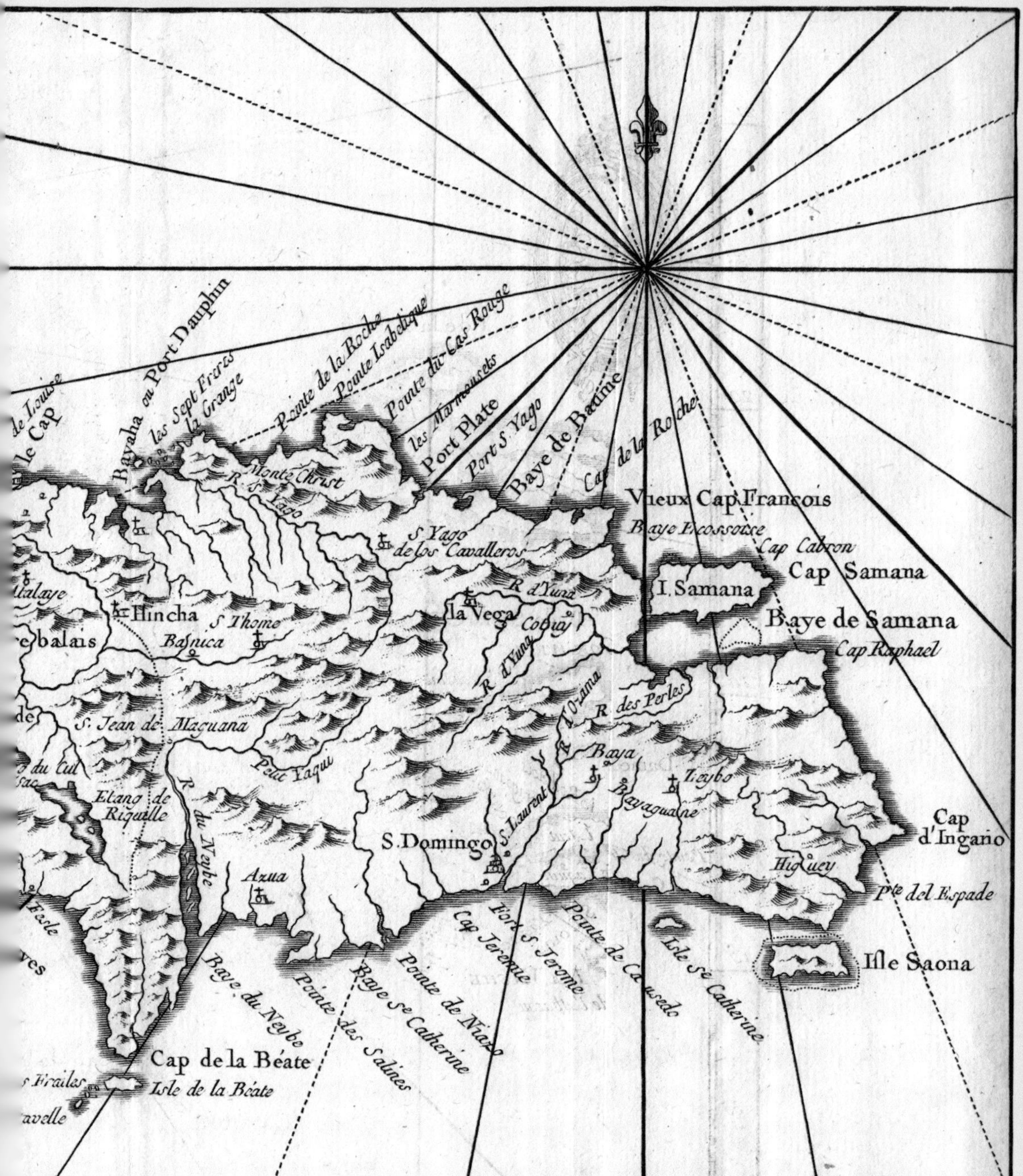

Bayaha ou Port Dauphin
les Sept Freres
la Grange
Pointe de la Roche
Pointe Isabelique
Pointe du Cas Rouge
les Marmousets
Port Plate
Port S. Yago
Cap de la Roche
Monte Christ
R. S. Yago
S. Yago de los Cavalleros
Vieux Cap Francois
Cap Cabron
Cap Samana
I. Samana
Baye de Samana
Cap Raphael
R. d'Yuna
la Vega
Cotuy
Hincha
S. Thome
Banica
S. Jean de Maguana
R. des Perles
R. d'Ozama
Petit Yaqui
Etang de Riquille
R. du Neybe
Baya
Bayaguane
Zeybo
S. Laurent
S. Domingo
Azua
Cap d'Ingano
Higuey
Pte del Espade
Isle Saona
Isle Ste Catherine
Pointe de Causedo
Port S. Jerome
Cap Jerome
Pointe de Niazo
Baye Ste Catherine
Pointe des Salines
Baye du Neybe
Cap de la Béate
Isle de la Béate
74
30
73
30
72
30
71
30

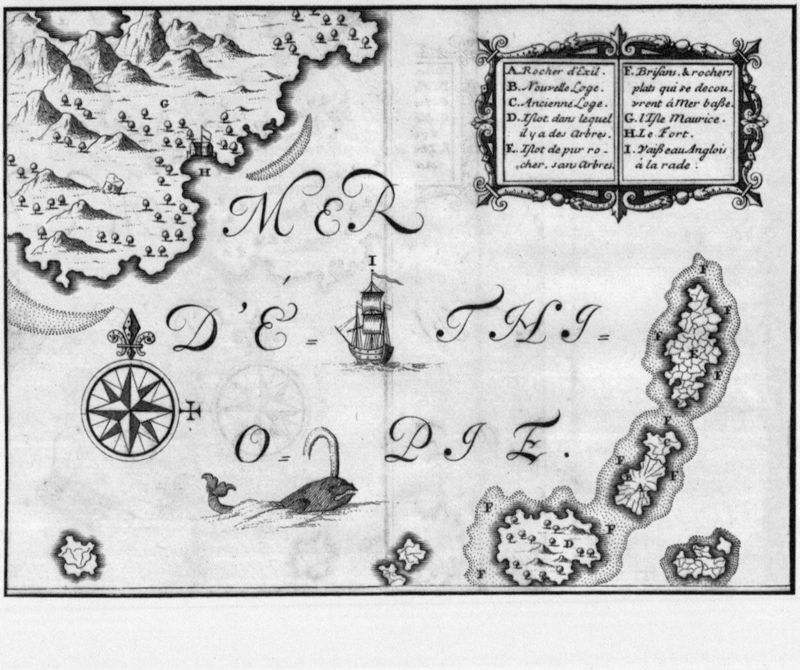

A. Rocher d'Exil.
B. Nouvelle Loge.
C. Ancienne Loge.
D. Islot. dans lequel il y a des Arbres.
E. Islot de pur rocher. sans Arbres.
F. Brisans. & rochers plats qui se decouvrent á Mer baße.
G. l'Isle Maurice.
H. Le Fort.
I. Vaißeau Anglois á la rade.
MER D'ÉTHIOPIE.

knives, and much else besides. According to Charles Johnson[4], when Drummond, some of his officers and sailors were ashore, Bowen and four of his cohorts, armed with pistols and cutlasses, managed to board the *Speedy Return* under pretext of doing trade. Using the element of surprise, and the fact that most of the sailors remaining on board were in the hold, they quickly succeeded in taking over the boat and signalled to the other 150 pirates who were ready and waiting to come on board. The *Content* was also captured and then burnt.

Captain Bowen and his men were soon back at sea, heading once again for Bourbon where, thanks to sheer weight of numbers, they managed to overturn Governor de Villers' ban on trade with pirates, purchasing water and food from the island's settlers on 19 August 1702.

At the end of August, Bowen weighed anchor, and spent some time cruising off Noordwester Haven (present-day Port Louis) before returning to Madagascar. By the end of December he was in Mayotte where he met up with Thomas Howard, with whom he had taken the *Speaker*. The two of them decided to join forces and, sailing together, they captured in March 1703 the East Indiaman *Pembroke*, commanded by Captain George Woolley.

In August that same year, they ransacked a number of small Indian and Arab boats in the Red Sea, accumulating a considerable amount of booty (equivalent to over US$113,000).

At the beginning of the following year, Bowen was back in Mauritius. On 6 February 1704, he entered the port of Frederik Hendrik (now Vieux

4. Charles Johnson is the credited author of *A General History of the Robberies and Murders of the Most Notorious Pyrates*, which appeared in England in 1724. Today, the book is usually attributed to Daniel Defoe, a pseudonym.

ABOVE: Ship's purser's strongbox. Pirates and privateers used these to stash their loot and precious personal belongings whenever they could lay their hands on them.
*'Nuremburg' strongbox, 18th century.*

OPPOSITE (TOP): Port Louis on Île Sainte Marie, just off Madagascar, viewed from the old monument which commemorates the French annexation of the island.
*Drawing by Bulluria, engraved by Couché and Fortier, 19th century.*

OPPOSITE (BOTTOM): Map drawn up by François Leguat in 1693, showing the location of the fort built by the Dutch where the governor Roelof Diodati resided. The *Speaker*, with John Bowen and his crew on board, was shipwrecked just a stone's throw from this fort in 1702.
*Illustration taken from* A New Voyage to the East-Indies *by François Leguat and his Companions..., Amsterdam, 1708.*

Grand Port) aboard the *Defiance*, a ship he had taken in the Red Sea and renamed, with a crew of over 100 pirates. The governor of Frederik Hendrik port, Abraham Momber van de Velde (1703–1710), and the island's small colony were on the alert even though they were painfully aware that they could offer little in the way of resistance if the pirates chose to attack. They were also somewhat puzzled as to the reason for the pirates' presence, and for their staying longer than expected.

Surprisingly, relations between the settlers and the pirates remained courteous throughout the latter's two-month stay on the island. All transactions were carried out in due form and fully paid for. On 5 April 1704, Captain Bowen weighed anchor and set sail for Île Bourbon where, after negotiations with Governor de Villers, he and several of his companions decided to lay down their arms and retire from piracy.

Marina Carter, in her book *Pirates of Mauritius*, gives a list of names of pirates who chose to become peaceful settlers: Guy Dumesnil, Robert Tarby (originally from Edinburgh), Thomas Elgar and Edward Robert (originally from London), George Noel and Joseph de Guigné[5] (originally from Saumur, France). Before these amnesties, other pirates such as Pierre Boisson, Jacques Naze and Jacques Pitou had already settled on Bourbon between 1701 and 1702. John Bowen, who never married and remained heirless, died suddenly "six months after settling on the island"[6]. Official records, made out by Governor de Villers, date his death to 17 March 1705.

**ABOVE:** On the east coast of Mauritius, at the Barachois de Belmont about 12 miles north of where the *Speaker* was shipwrecked, one can see the letters "jen Bow n" then an "e", and then "de pacqu", all carved into a rock. Was this inscription carved by one of John Bowen's men when they were on the island in 1702 for three months, or perhaps during their two-month stay in 1704? Does it, considered together with other carved signs, lead to a treasure buried nearby? (In this photo, the grooves carved into the volcanic rock have been highlighted in chalk to make them more visible.)

**OPPOSITE:** View over Fort Frederik Hendrik, southeast of Mauritius, in 1642, 60 years before John Bowen was shipwrecked in the area in January 1702. The hazards of having to share an island with pirates were among the factors which prompted the Dutch authorities in Cape Town to abandon their attempts to settle on the island.

*Document taken from* Le Premier Établissement des Néerlandais à Maurice, *Prince Roland Bonaparte, Paris, 1890.*

## Life with the Brethren of the Coast in Madagascar

At the beginning of the 17th century, the freebooters of the West Indies formed an association that they called the Brethren of the Coast, a loose brotherhood of outlaws and outcasts who terrorise the Caribbean Sea.

Though the Brethren was chased out of the region at the end of the 17th century, its more tenacious members, such as Every, Bowen, Burgess, Halsey, White and Howard, settled in the north of Madagascar (known at the time as Île Saint Laurent), particularly on Île Sainte Marie. These English and French pirates replaced the said Dutch freebooters, and set about discovering the pleasures of the tropical climate of the Malagasy coast. The local inhabitants willingly traded with them, which meant that the pirates were abundantly supplied in fish and meat.

Then, at the beginning of the 18th century other pirates, such as Condent, Taylor, England, Davis, Misson and Le Vasseur, arrived to take advantage of

5. Could the shipwrecked passenger of the *Saint-Géran* (1744, see p. 122), Pierre de Guigné, be the grandson of Joseph de Guigné the pirate?

6. Auguste Toussaint, *Dictionnaire de Biographie Mauricienne/Dictionary of Mauritian Biography*, journal No. 14, July 1944, p. 419.

TOP: The Petit Fort du Nord (left) and Île aux Prunes (right).

MIDDLE: The Chiefs' House (left) and Grand Fort Hovas (right).

BOTTOM: Tamatave and Tamatave Point.

*East coast of Madagascar, engravings by Èvremont de Bérard, circa 1880.*

EV. DE BERARD

## Aboard

A pirate ship's essential crew was composed of Europeans: English, French, Dutch, Danish and Swedish, sailing alongside often-large numbers of Indians and slaves who were captured and then released. The number of people on board was frequently two or three times that of a classic merchant ship. They would sleep wherever they could, usually on the bare boards of the lower decks.

Members of the crew who played musical instruments would form a band. During battles, they would accompany the action with warlike hymns on drums and trumpets, or they would play sinister tunes designed to trouble the enemies' spirit and demoralise them. Mainly, though, the band's role was to enliven the frequent orgiastic feasts and the even more frequent rum- and wine-drinking sessions.

During marauding campaigns, which sometimes lasted months, daily life on board for the pirates consisted mainly of maintaining the ship: scrubbing decks, repairing rigging, pumping out bilges, mending sails and cleaning their wide range of weapons and artillery. The latter included cutlasses, daggers, dirks and assorted knives, marlinspikes, axes, muskets, pistols, blunderbusses, swivel guns or *petereros*, *grenadoes* (grenades), cannons, various types of cannonballs, grapeshot, grappling hooks and caltrops, and anything else that they had come across during their raids.

The captain was elected by the crew, and was chosen for his navigation and leadership skills, as well as for his boldness and courage. He also needed to be cunning and ferocious to the point of cruelty. Although he occupied a spacious cabin, and used fine chinaware and silver for his meals, a captain could, at any time, be interrupted by a crewman who wanted to talk.

It was during battle that the captain was really able to exercise his full powers, to the extent of killing his own shipmates if they disobeyed orders.

Each crewman had to sign the ship's articles, a charter constituting a code of conduct which the pirates were obliged to follow.

In effect, life on board was governed by a hierarchical system founded on elements of democracy. Directly under the orders of the captain was the quartermaster or boatswain, who was also elected by the crew and, therefore, just as easily voted out by them. Consequently, the quartermaster represented the collective will of the crew, and the captain could not easily act without his concord.

Two or three officers would be nominated by agreement between the captain and the quartermaster, and placed under the latter's command. Sometimes an officer would be designated as second-in-command, in case the captain was killed in the midst of a boarding or sea battle.

The quartermaster oversaw provisions and the general running of the ship. For this he had under his direct authority people such as the master gunner, the master carpenter, the master sail-maker and the ship's surgeon. In the absence of a surgeon to tend to injuries and perform amputations, these jobs would fall upon the carpenter.

the bays and coves of Madagascar's northeast coast[7] and the Île Sainte Marie as convenient havens where they could carry out necessary repairs.

The port of Sainte Marie, in the southwest of the little island, was protected from the trade winds and cyclones, and could easily harbour around 20 ships. There, the pirates traded slaves, buying and then reselling them to European visitors.

Some of the pirates learnt the local language and served as interpreters for people passing through. Others settled more permanently on the island, marrying a local girl (if not several). Between pillaging campaigns in the Indian Ocean or the Red Sea, they would return home to their families and live in more-or-less-developed settlements or even fortified villages.

On Île Sainte Marie, the story is told of James Plantain, an English pirate

7. Diégo Suarez, Antongil, Nosy Mangabe, Masselage, Boina, Mahajamba, Fénérive, Bombetoka, Foulpointe, Ambanivolo, Tintingue, Rantabe, Pointe à Larée…

ABOVE: Tintingue Bay, on the east coast of Madagascar, was a popular pirate haunt in the early 18th century.

*Drawing by Bullaria, engraved by Couché, France Pittoresque, 1830.*

OPPOSITE: (Detail) Radama I (1793–1828), King of Madagascar from 1810 to 1828. He made Antananarivo (formerly Tananarive) the capital of the Kingdom of Madagascar. He was the uncle of Ratsitatane, son of Andriamambavola, the minister of the King.

*Engraving drawn by Collignon, engraved by Lechard, taken from* Voyage autour du Monde, *19th century.*

born in Jamaica, who, especially fond of members of the fairer sex, had assembled himself a harem. It is said he used to adorn his women with the very best jewels and the finest of fineries, while also taking great care to keep them away from his covetous fellow scoundrels.

However, the days in which a pirate could live as a kinglet were numbered. In 1721, a well-armed squadron under the command of Commodore Matthews arrived on the scene, and contributed to gradually stamping out piracy in the region.

## Christopher Condent (?–1734)

Christopher Condent (also spelt as Congdom, Congon and Condon, amongst others) was born in Plymouth, but it is not known exactly when. He began his nautical career serving as a quartermaster on an American 12-gun sloop, during which time he once single-handedly fought and killed an Indian crewman who was threatening to blow up the ship. Soon after this incident, the sloop captured the *Duke of York*, a merchantman. After a dispute, the crew was split between the two ships, with Condent being elected captain of the sloop.

Around 1718, the newly-appointed governor of the Bahamas, Commodore Woodes Rogers, was given the task of ridding the Caribbean of pirates. Condent took the hint and fled Providence Island for Cape Verde, where he seized a merchant ship carrying wines from Madeira.

On an excursion across the Atlantic to the coasts of Brazil, he took several new prizes and adopted the practice of cutting off the ears and noses of his Portuguese prisoners. Back in the Cape Verde archipelago, around the island of Maio, he continued to wreak havoc, taking an entire flotilla of some 20 ships, before heading for the island of St. Jago (now Santiago). There he took over a Dutch ship and renamed it the *Flying Dragon*.

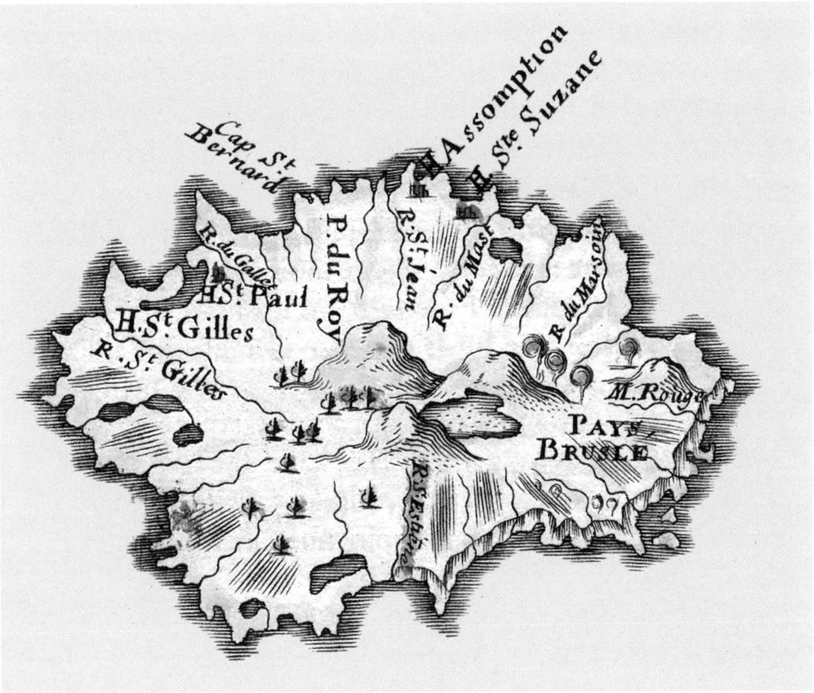


Success followed success: first, an English prize, the *Wright*, commanded by a Captain Spelt, then a Portuguese ship, and then a 26-gun Dutch vessel. Leaving the *Wright* behind, and in charge of a fleet of three boats loaded with precious loot, Condent set sail for the seas off the Gold Coast (present-day Ghana), where again prize followed prize: the *Indian Queen*, the *Fame*, and another Dutch ship.

In July 1719, Condent headed for the Indian Ocean, where his luck continued to hold: there he captured an English East Indiaman, the *George*, a vessel from Ostend, the *Prince Eugene*, and then, off the coast of Bombay, in 1720, he took over a magnificent Arab vessel on which he found a haul of precious objects worth an estimated US$232,000 (by today's value).

Christopher Condent and 32 of his men settled on Île Bourbon in February 1721, having been granted amnesty by the governor, Beauvollier de Courchant. Only a dozen of the pirates ended up staying on the island, becoming, in time, peaceful settlers.

*Map of Île Bourbon taken from* Description de l'Univers, *Alain Manesson Mallet, 1683.*

ABOVE: An 18th-century mode of transport – an exotic version of the sedan chair used in France – on Île Bourbon.

*Drawing by Danvin, engraved by L.Berlié, 19th century.*

OPPOSITE: From 1685 to 1730, pirates based on Île Sainte Marie often sailed to the Comoros to the northwest of Madagascar, sometimes for stays of a few days or weeks.

*Map taken from* Description de l'Univers, *Alain Manesson Mallet, 1683.*

That same year, after this run of success, Condent decided to head for Île Sainte Marie off the coast of Madagascar, the main lair of the Indian Ocean pirates. There, he linked up with the pirates John Halsey and Edward England, and together they carried out an audacious attack on an English East Indiaman named the *Cassandra* commanded by Captain Macrae[8].

After they had shared out the impressive booty from the *Cassandra*, Condent returned to Île Sainte Marie, where he decided to put an end to his life of piracy and retire with his loot. He asked Captain Baker, commander of a small English vessel called the *Cooker*, to take a message to the governor of Île Bourbon, Beauvollier de Courchant, requesting amnesty for himself and his 35 men (accompanied by 60 slaves), indicating that all of them were

8. In 1725, Captain Macrae was appointed Governor of Madras (now Chennai), an English stronghold in India. He remained in this post until 1730.

87
COSTES D'ABEX D'AIAN ET DE ZANGUEBAR
EGYPTE
NUBIE
ARABIE
MER ROUGE
Coste d'Abex
Suaquem
Mazuan
Arquico
Zama
Nil R
Destroit de Bebel Mendel
C. Guardafu
Isle de Zocotora
MER
Mette
Dardara
Felles M.
Zeila
Dangali
Dangali
Soalai
Zingi
ABISSINIE
Montagne
Dalli
Coste d'Aian
Arum
Mer
DES
de
INDES
Adel
Adea
Coste
Opin
Magadoxo
Braua
Orient
Occident
Ligne
Æquinoctialle
Pale
Zanguebar
Melinde
Monbaze
Ganze
Montagne de
Atonda
Coste de Zanguebar
I. Pemba
I. Zanzibar
I. Monfia
I. de Iuan Miz
I de Castre
I. Comore
Quiloa
Mogulo
Angoch
Mozambique
Cap Delgado
CAFRES
Isle de Madagascar
I Natal
I de l'Arque
Abrolho I
I de St Francisco
I de Gale
60
65
70
75
80
20
15
10
5
Midy

willing to become "good and loyal subjects of the King of France". The governor and his council met on 25 November 1720 and decided to grant Condent's request on the conditions that he and his men relinquish their arms to the authorities on their arrival, that each man be accompanied by no more than one slave, and that each man pay a fee of 20 piastres. Condent and 32 of his pirates accepted these conditions, and they arrived in Île Bourbon in February 1721.

Two months later, in April, following the taking of the *Nossa Senhora do Cabo (Our Lady of the Cape)*, Condent contributed successfully to the negotiations between Olivier Le Vasseur, John Taylor and the governor of Île Bourbon which resulted in the release of the Count of Ericeira in exchange

## Boarding tactics

Pirates' weapons, apart from shipboard weapons, were often limited to cutlasses, muskets, daggers, pistols and marlinspikes. Their number, courage, ferocity and sheer greed had to do the rest.

Trickery and deceit were among the most common tactics used before an attack. A classic ruse consisted of displaying a friendly flag, then, at the opportune moment, running up the Jolly Roger to the general consternation of the crew of the targeted vessel, who found themselves suddenly faced with a boarding by bloodthirsty pirates.

Another common trick was for a number of the crew to hide, giving the impression that, with so few people on board, the ship was harmless. In a similar vein, some of the pirates would disguise themselves as women in order to fool the enemy and allay suspicion.

Another subterfuge involved artificially inducing the pirate boat to list (to tilt to much in one direction) and then sending out distress signals. The coveted ship, naively coming to the aid of its co-mariners, would find itself alongside a pirate ship being cleared for action stations and bristling with frenzied cutthroats, armed to the teeth and about to board.

The prize would then be thoroughly searched and stripped of its cargo and valuables. This booty was shared out between the pirates in accordance with the articles signed by each crewmember. Those who resisted the pirates were tortured or killed, and their bodies summarily thrown overboard. If, by chance, an ex-Royal Navy sailor should recognise a captain or officer who had abused his authority over him, he would take full advantage of the situation to exact vengeance.

Once the enemy ship was under the pirate captain's control, he could choose to take command of it, entrust it to one of his men, burn it, or simply abandon it.

OPPOSITE: (Detail) The taking of a Spanish galleon by pirates in the Caribbean in the 16th century.
*19th century engraving taken from* L'Univers Illustré, *Michel Lévy frères, Paris.*

## Pirate strategies

Pirates relied on networks of spies operating in the ports they frequented to tip them off about merchant convoys, their routes, their armaments and, of course, their cargoes. These informers were naturally well-rewarded for their work.

Pirate captains were experienced seamen who had a profound knowledge of the sea and naval navigation. They preferred to use boats that were easy to manoeuvre, such as sloops or brigantines. On the high seas, they favoured small two-masted frigates, armed with a dozen or so cannons. These boats could sail considerably faster than those of the various East India companies, which tended to be large and ponderous. This enabled the pirates to get close to these impressive vessels while they were going about, hence avoiding their devastating broadsides.

During approach manoeuvres, while still out of range of cannon shot, pirates would vociferate, bellow insults, brandish their cutlasses, and fire their muskets to frighten and demoralise the enemy crew who were usually a lot less willing to die than the pirates. The pirate ship's final approach and the rapidity of engagement were crucial to the success of an attack. Often, the captain's choice of the precise moment to board would determine the outcome of the battle.

OPPOSITE (TOP AND BOTTOM): Of Irish origin, Edward England was probably the only pirate who forgo torture. He even went so far as to show goodwill to Captain Macrae, the future Governor of Madras. England's associates, Taylor and Le Vasseur were unable to forgive this sign of weakness and marooned him on the almost-deserted Île de France along with three faithful companions.
*Engravings, 18th century (top) and 1725 (below).*

PAGE 50: (Detail) Pirates boarding – a rare moment of intense excitement and danger during which lives were constantly under threat from blade and bullet. Daring, courage and the fury to win were the only ways to survive.
*19th century drawing by Moraine, engraved by Ferdinand.*

PAGE 51: Campaigning along the Malabar Coast, Edward England captured several small Indian boats, as well as bigger Dutch, English and Belgian ones.
*18th century engraving, drawn and engraved by Bernard.*

for a modest ransom[9]. In November 1721, 20 of the 32 pirates left the island for Europe. After a peaceful year living on Île Bourbon, Condent sailed for France on board the *Vierge de Grès*, commanded by Captain Jacques Jonchée de La Golletterie, leaving behind a son, Jean-Baptiste Condon (Condent is said to have married the governor's sister-in-law).

He settled in Brittany at Port Louis, married Catherine Ancré, a good lady from Lorient, and spent a dozen years as a respectable shipowner under the name of Edouard Congdon. He died in 1734.

### Edward England (?–1720)

It is not known when or where Edward England was born, although it is generally assumed to be sometime around 1685. He was of Irish origin, and his real name was Edward Seegar.

9. See p. 58.

His pirating career began in 1717, on board a Jamaican sloop which was taken in the Bahamas by the pirate Captain Christopher Winter. Although initially forced into piracy, England fit in well, and was popular enough with his co-marauders to be elected as captain of another sloop that they had captured. At this time, the war that Commodore Woodes Rogers was waging against the pirates had become so intense that those who refused to accept the amnesty proffered by the British Crown[10] decided to flee the region, England amongst them. He set sail for the west coast of Africa where he captured the *Cadogan*, commanded by Captain Skinner, which he entrusted to his fellow pirate Howell Davis. England then seized the *Pearl*, which he renamed the *Royal James*, and became its captain. He then continued to sweep the seas off the coasts of Africa with a crew that was totally devoted to him.

Unlike most of his peers, England was not a cruel man; he did not approve of torture and only used it in extreme cases.

In 1719, with the *Royal James* under his command, England's ingenuity was rewarded with a dozen prizes including the *Elisabeth and Katherine* and the *Mercury*, which he renamed the *Queen Ann's Revenge* and the *Flying King* and gave to Captains Lane and Sample respectively, both of whom decided to return to the Caribbean. Captain England, however, remained, and attacked in quick succession the *Peterborough*, which he kept for himself, and the *Victory*, which he abandoned. Heading south along the African coast, after failing to capture a couple of ships off Cape Corso on the Gold Coast, he attempted to pillage Whydah (Ouida in modern-day Benin), only to find that it had already been stripped of anything worth taking by Olivier Le Vasseur.

10. In order to curb piracy and its ravages in the Caribbean, the king of Great Britain, George I, decreed amnesty for those who were willing to lay down their arms.

PETITS BATIMENTS INDIENS,
en uſage ſur la côte de Malabar.

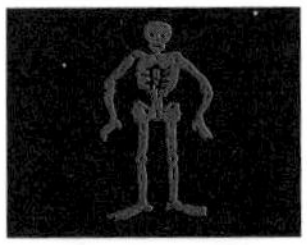

1

2

3

4

5

6

7

8

9

## The Jolly Roger

The Jolly Roger is a black flag with a skull and crossbones motif, infamously used by pirate ships about to attack. There are several accounts of its origins.

One version goes back to the 16th century, when a black flag was hoisted to the top of a mast in order to signal that plague carriers were on board the ship. A white cross was then placed on the black background, which morphed into the crossed tibias to which the skull was later added.

Another version comes from England, also in the 16th century: the word "roger" had the meaning of "vagabond" and, at the beginning of the 18th century, "Old Roger" was a term for the Devil. Thus, it is not impossible that Jolly Roger means "diabolic vagabond of the seas", a fitting name for a pirate's flag.

The third version, probably the most widespread, takes us to the Caribbean and the buccaneers who were the first to hoist a red flag to indicate that no quarter would be given, in other words, "death to all who resist". Pirates, many of them being French, knew this flag as the "Joli Rouge", meaning "pretty red". It does not take much phonetic deformation to get from there to "Jolly Roger" in English. Over time, as the term became more widespread, the colour changed and the bones were added.

With the number of pirates increasing and their infamy spreading in the Caribbean, the most dangerous pirates wanted to personalise their flags, mainly in order to be recognised on their approach and thus spread terror on board the enemy ship. The symbols used on these flags reminded the hapless victims that refusal to surrender would mean death.

The most notorious Jolly Rogers of the period were those of captains Henry Every, Christopher Condent, Edward England, Ned Low, Edward Teach and Thomas Tew. Christopher Moody, a pirate captain who gave no quarter, had a Jolly Roger with a red background instead of the usual black.

After a break of several months, in the port of Nova Sofala in the Kingdom of Mutapa (present-day Zimbabwe and Mozambique), England confusingly renamed the *Peterborough* the *Victory*.

At the beginning of 1720, after some more time spent holed up in a bay in the north of Madagascar, England sailed for the Malabar Coast in the company of John Taylor. The hunt was profitable: some small Indian craft, a Dutch 44-gun vessel, which he renamed the *Fancy* and incorporated into his small squadron, two English boats and an Indiaman from the Ostend Company. One of the two English ships, the *Cassandra*, commanded by Captain Macrae, put up more resistance than usual. A furious battle raged for many hours. 90 pirates were killed or wounded, and on the English side 13 were killed and 80 wounded. Eventually, the marauders came out victorious and took possession of booty worth an estimated US$117,000. The *Fancy*, however, was in a sorry state, having suffered greatly from Macrae's intense broadsides, so England appropriated the *Cassandra* for himself. John Taylor was eager to execute Macrae to avenge the dead and wounded pirates. Despite this, England decided to release Macrae and his crew, allowing them to stay on the shattered remains of the *Fancy*, along with some of their merchandise.

This act of indulgence, however, would cost England dearly. After a stopover in Madagascar, Taylor and Le Vasseur marooned England along with three others in true pirate fashion on Île de France (present-day Mauritius, which at the time was still almost a desert island). The four of them spent the next few months hard at work building a small boat, on which they eventually set off for Madagascar. Setting the example for Captain Bligh of the *Bounty* some 70 years later, England and his companions managed to sail across 932 miles of the Indian Ocean in what was little more than a rowing boat. They finally arrived in the bay of Saint Augustin on the west coast of Madagascar, exactly where, in 1602, the French had first set foot on the island. England lived out his days among his fellow pirates and in utter destitution, begging for a living until his death towards the end of 1720.

OPPOSITE: Pirates' personal flags.
1. Edward Low.
2. Edward Teach, known as Blackbeard.
3. Bartholomew Roberts' first flag.
4. Edward England.
5. Emmanuel Wynne.
6. Bartholomew Roberts' second flag.
7. Christopher Moody.
8. Thomas Tew, possible grandfather of Queen Bety.
9. Christopher Condent.

BELOW: A 17th-century French Navy sea chest and cutlass.
*L'Échoppe marine, Village Suisse, Paris.*

## Olivier Le Vasseur (1680–1730)

Olivier Le Vasseur, otherwise known as La Bouche, La Buse and The Buzzard, among other aliases, was born in Calais around 1680. His mother passed away after childbirth, leaving him in the hands of a wet nurse and a corsair father, Paul Le Vasseur, who taught him the secrets of navigation.

ABOVE: (Detail) Pirates rarely sat for portraits. Most portraits of pirates, therefore, are works of imagination that do not necessarily resemble their subjects. Nevertheless, it is perfectly plausible that the best-known of the Mascarene pirates, Olivier Le Vasseur, would have looked something like this.
*Drawing by Moraine, engraved by Ferdinand, 19th century.*

OPPOSITE: Goa, stronghold of the Portuguese in India in the 17th century, was the capital of the Kingdom of Visapoor, which bordered the Kingdom of Golconda. Count Ericeira, the Portuguese Viceroy of India, left Goa on board a ship of the Portuguese East India Company, in charge of a fabled treasure trove intended for the Portuguese Crown.
*Map drawn up by R. de Vaugondy, Paris, 1749.*

PAGES 56 & 57: The Bay of Saint-Paul on Île Bourbon where the Portuguese ship Nossa Senhora do Cabo was attacked by Olivier Le Vasseur and John Taylor in April 1721.

In records, Le Vasseur reappears in 1714 and 1716 in the West Indies alongside Captain Benjamin Hornigold and Edward Teach, the infamous Blackbeard, and then with the English captain Samuel Bellamy, from whom he split away in 1717. Le Vasseur consorted with Providence Island pirates in the Bahamas, until Commodore Woodes Rogers turned up in 1718 with his offer of amnesty or elimination. Le Vasseur took the third option and sailed off to the West African coast in the company of Edward England. In 1720, not far from the Gambian coast, hc mct and tcamcd up with Howell Davis and, along with another pirate, Thomas Cocklyn, they scoured the seas off Sierra Leone.

After a rest at the pirate lair in the bay of Ambodifotatra on Île Sainte Marie just off Madagascar, Captain Le Vasseur assumed command of the *Indian Queen*, a fine 250-tonner vessel armed with 24 cannons and carrying a crew of 90 men. Le Vasseur wrecked the *Indian Queen* at Mayotte, where he encountered John Taylor who offered him the command of one of his ships, the *Victory*. In concert with Taylor, who commanded the *Defiance*, and Edward England, in charge of the *Cassandra*, Le Vasseur sailed for Île de France where he and Taylor marooned England for his release of Captain Macrae. Taylor and Le Vasseur then embarked on a fruitful campaign around the Indian coasts before returning to Île de France in February 1721 to re-supply and repair their boats. It was then that, according to the historian Auguste Toussaint[11], they carved the following inscription on a tree by the shoreline: "Left this place 4 April to go to Madagascar." Since then they sailed for Île Bourbon, and the reason for the change in destination is not known.

11. Auguste Toussaint, *Dictionnaire de biographie mauricienne*, bulletin No. 12, December 1943, p. 362

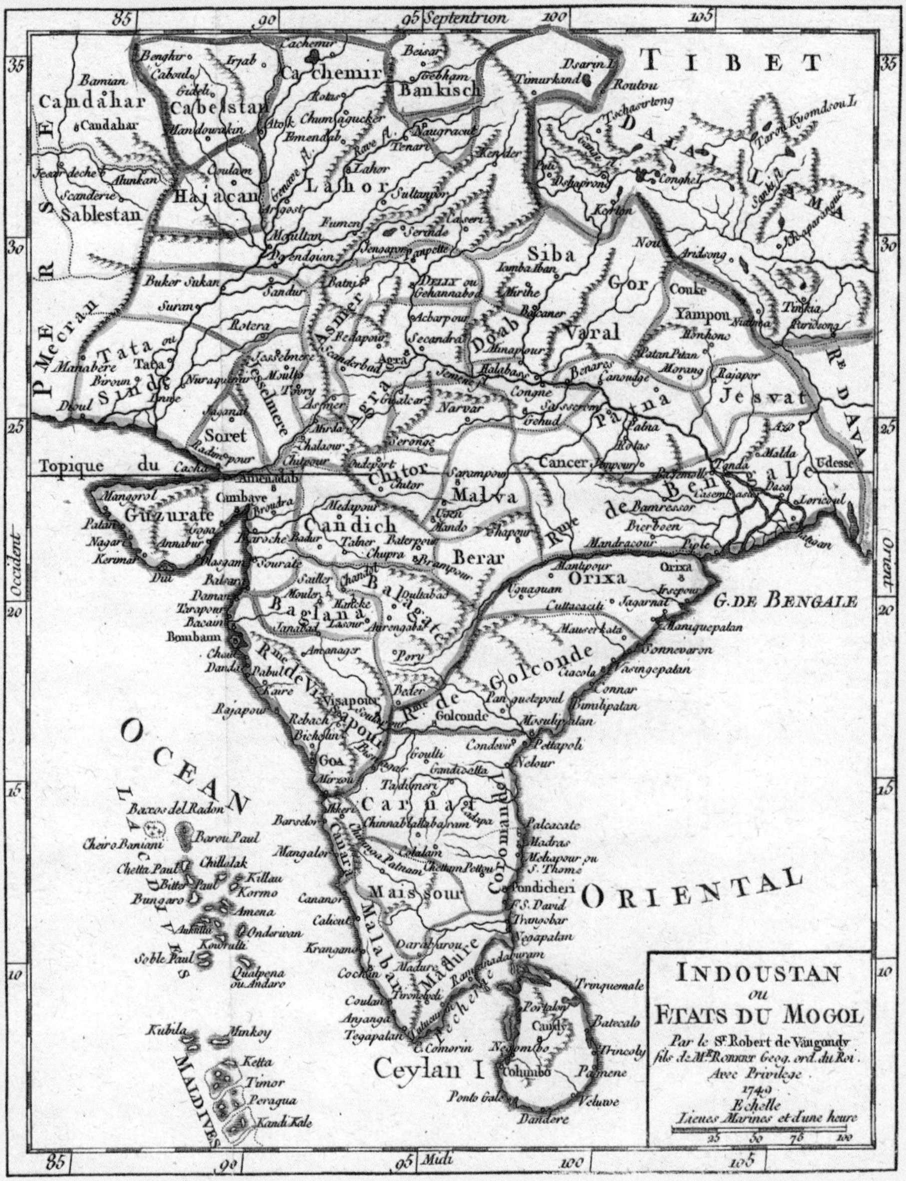

INDOUSTAN
ou
ETATS DU MOGOL
Par le Sr. Robert de Vaugondy
fils de Mr. Robert Geog. ord. du Roi.
Avec Privilege
1749
Echelle
Lieues Marines et d'une heure
25 50 75 100
Septentrion
Midi
Occident
Orient
85
90
95
100
105
35
30
25
20
15
10
TIBET
DALAI LAMA
R. DE DAVA
PERSE
Mecran
Candahar
Cabelstan
Cachemir
Bankisch
Hajacan
Sablestan
Lahor
Siba
Gor
Varal
Doab
Asmer
Agra
Tata ou Sinde
Soret
Jesselmere
Patna
Jesvat
Bengale
Topique du Cancer
Guzurate
Candich
Chitor
Malva
Berar
Orixa
Baglana
Balagate
Golconde
R.me de Visapour
R.me de Golconde
G. DE BENGALE
OCEAN ORIENTAL
Carnate
Maissour
Malabar
Madure
Coromandel
Ceylan I
LACDIVES
MALDIVES
Delly ou Gehannabad
Agra
Amenadab
Cambaye
Bombaim
Goa
Golconde
Visapour
Pondicheri
Madras
Meliapour ou S. Thomé
Candy
Columbo
C. Comorin

There, in the harbour of Saint-Paul, on the morning of 8 April 1721, Le Vasseur and Taylor came across a magnificent 72-gun vessel belonging to the Portuguese East India Company. The *Nossa Senhora do Cabo* (Our Lady of the Cape; also known as the *Virgem do Cabo*, the Virgin of the Cape), as it was called, was a Dutch ship that had been sold to the Portuguese Crown, and was being repaired after a rough encounter with a cyclone. The two pirates could not resist such easy prey. Le Vasseur in the *Victory* took the port side of the Portuguese boat and Taylor in the *Defiance* went to starboard. Up went the Jolly Roger and away they blasted with cannon and musket. Panic reigned among the Portuguese ranks, with several being killed in the crossfire.

The few dozen surviving crewmen on board quickly struck the Portuguese colours and surrendered. The remainder of the 130 crew were ashore, together with the ship's illustrious passengers, Dom Luís Carlos Inácio Xavier de Meneses (Count of Ericeira and Portuguese Viceroy of India) and Dom Sebastian de Andrado (Archbishop of Goa). They were in the company of the governor, Joseph Beauvollier de Courchant, his assistant, Antoine Desforges-Boucher, and the captain of the *Nossa Senhora do Cabo*. On board his recent prize, Le Vasseur discovered a treasure trove beyond his or most people's wildest dreams, that the viceroy was taking to the rivers of diamonds from the Kingdoms of Golkonda and Visapoor, ingots of gold and silver, chests full of pearls, furniture in rare woods, ebony and rosewood, as well as sacred objects and the solid gold cross of the Archbishop of Goa, which was studded with rubies and weighed close to 220 pounds (lbs). All of whose worth added up, at the time, to an estimated 900,000 British Pound Sterling – nearly the equivalent of over US$1,500,000 today; it was almost certainly one of the biggest pirate hauls in the Indian Ocean.

According to Jacob de Bucquoy[12], Taylor ordered the Count of Ericeira be brought back on board. There, in tears, the Count handed his diamond- and emerald-studded gold sword to Taylor, who returned it saying: "Keep it; I bequeath it to you in memory of your unfortunate fate." There is another version of this story, involving a Frenchman named Duval[13] who claimed to have got the story from the Count himself. In this version, the Count returned to his ship and fought at the head of his men. However, the 200 pirates soon chased off the Portuguese sailors who all jumped into the sea, leaving the Count with just 20 men and three loyal servants. At this point, Duval claims, Taylor saved the Count's life by calling a halt to the struggle.

Negotiations for the Count's ransom, which involved the governor and Christopher Condent, were long and eventually, Le Vasseur and Taylor finally agreed to a modest ransom, a mere 2,000 piastres, in exchange for the Count.

Loath to let a good opportunity slip by, Le Vasseur and Taylor also took the *Ville d'Ostende*, which was preparing to enter the port. Captain Le Vasseur, now in command of the *Nossa Senhora do Cabo*, then sailed off to his haunt in Madagascar, loaded down with his fabulous treasures and 60,000 *livres tournois* (well over US$100,000 in today's money), which he shared out with Taylor and his men.

The Count was obliged to stay on Île Bourbon a while longer, not least because he had to wait for Captain Garnier du Fougeray (who was to take him to France aboard the *Triton*) to take possession of the island in the name

12. In his book *Sous le Signe de la Tortue*, Albert Lougnon writes that Jacob de Bucquoy, a Dutch hydrographer, was taken prisoner by John Taylor following an attack on a Dutch settlement at Delagoa (now Maputo) on the African coast, and that Taylor had recounted to him the taking of the *Nossa Senhora do Cabo*, following which the hydrographer produced a detailed report.

13. François Duval, *Lettres curieuses sur divers sujets*, Paris, 1725.

OPPOSITE: It was at Saint-Paul that Olivier Le Vasseur was imprisoned, tried and hanged "high and short" in 1730.

PAGE 60 (TOP): (Detail) The map that belonged to Philippe Chevreau de Montléhu, a Mauritian treasure hunter who searched and excavated the Barachois de Belmont for 20 years without success.

PAGE 60 (BOTTOM): Le Vasseur's famous cryptogram. It has yet to be deciphered.

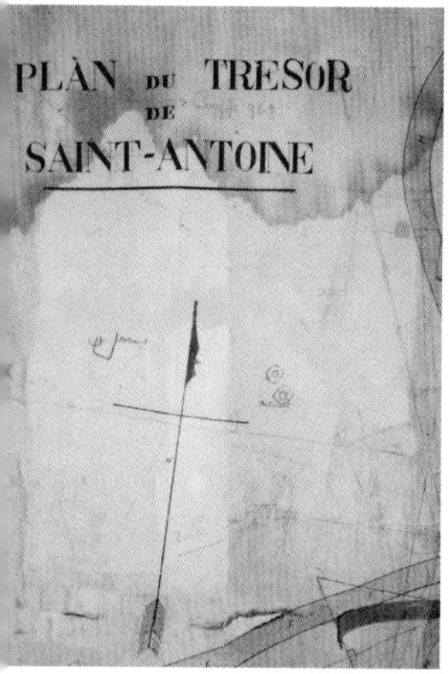

of France for the second time[14]. The *Triton* reached his destination on 23 March 1723 and Captain Garnier du Fougeray was made a Knight of the Order of Christ by the King of Portugal for his services.

Once in Madagascar, Le Vasseur renamed the *Nossa Senhora do Cabo* the *Victorieux* and set off hunting again with Taylor. This time, they took a magnificent French East India Company vessel, the *Duchesse de Noailles*, commanded by Captain Gravé. Le Vasseur and Taylor then had a serious argument which ended with them splitting up, with Taylor going back to thc Caribbean and Le Vasseur heading off for Madagascar.

In 1724, the governor of Île Bourbon, Desforges-Boucher, made all pirates an offer of general amnesty. Le Vasseur declined, but nevertheless sent him the sacred objects taken from the *Nossa Senhora do Cabo*. In December of the same year, Le Vasseur declined a further offer of amnesty despite its acceptance by some of his co-pirates such as John Clayton, Joseph Pascale (from La Rochelle), Adam Johnson and Guillaume Planter, all of whom settled on Bourbon. Desforges-Boucher died in 1725, and was replaced in January 1727 by Pierre Benoît Dumas, ex-member of the Supreme Council of Pondicherry. By this time, piracy was on the wane in the Indian Ocean, and the new governor had no love for the few remaining pirates. In 1730, he ordered Captain L'Hermitte, commander of the *Méduse*, to sail for Île Sainte Marie to capture Le Vasseur. Le Vasseur was imprisoned in the village of Saint-Paul on 26 April 1730. He was interrogated on 15 and 20 May, and again on 3 July, after which he was declared guilty of piracy and condemned to be hanged.

OPPOSITE: (Detail) Map of Madagascar showing the favourable location of Île Sainte Marie, a popular pirate lair, just a few nautical miles from the haven of the Bay of Antongil.
*Paris, late 18th century.*

---

14. On 20 September 1715, Captain Guillaume Dufresne d'Arsel took possession of Mauritius in the name of Louis XIV, changing the island's name to Île de France. On 23 September 1721, Captain Jean-Baptiste Garnier du Fougeray effected a second "taking possession" ceremony to reinforce French ownership of the island.

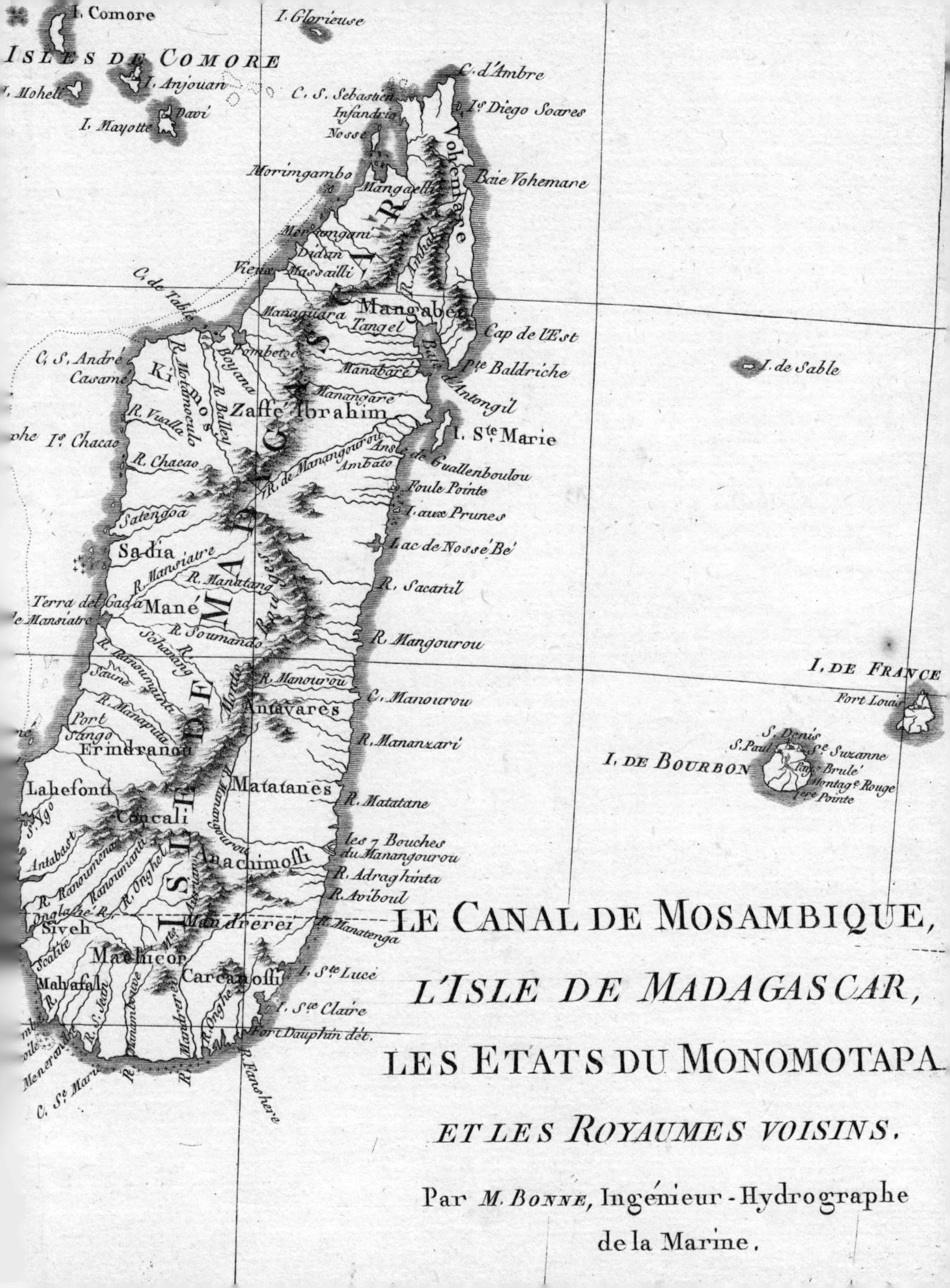


# LE CANAL DE MOSAMBIQUE, L'ISLE DE MADAGASCAR, LES ETATS DU MONOMOTAPA ET LES ROYAUMES VOISINS.

Par M. BONNE, Ingénieur-Hydrographe de la Marine.

## The judgement of Le Vasseur, according to Governor Dumas (according to the deliberations of the Superior Council of 7th July 1730):

By virtue of the Council, the extraordinary criminal trial carried out and instructed at the behest and diligence of the Procurer General of the King [unreadable] and accusation against Olivier Le Vasseur otherwise known as La Bouse [*sic*], accused of the crime of piracy, prisoner in our prisons, defendant of the statement[s] made on 26th March and 19th May by Sieur L'Hermitte captain of the ship the *Méduse*, the letter of the said Le Vasseur dated 25th March 1724 addressed to Monsieur Desforges signed Olivier La Buse, authenticated by him, signed and initialled, without modification. Letter of the Superior Council to Sieur La Buse in reply dated 23rd September of the same year granting amnesty and personal guarantees, interrogation endured by the accused on 15th and 20th May 1730 and on the 3rd of the present month. First general conclusion of the King of the 4th, preparatory judgement of the same day which ordains that it shall be taken as the definitive judgement given the public notoriety. Final conclusion of the Procurer General of the King of the 6th, interrogation carried out in the chamber of the Council [unreadable] and all things considered the Council has declared and [unreadable] the aforenamed Olivier Le Vasseur otherwise known as La Buse native of Calais gravely tainted by the cognizance of the crime of piracy over a period of several years, of having commanded several pirate vessels having taken and taken off from the port of Île Bourbon a vessel belonging to the King of Portugal and another named the *Ville d'Ostende* belonging to the Company of the same town but equally participating in the taking of, plundering and burning of the vessel the *Duchesse de Noailles* belonging to the Company of France and other [unreadable], for reparation of which the Council has condemned him to make honourable amends before the main door of the church of this parish, naked in his shirt, a rope around his neck, in his hand a flaming torch of four pounds and there to say and declare in a loud and intelligible voice that wickedly and recklessly he has for several years pursued the trade of pirate for which he repents and asks pardon from God, from the King and from justice. This done [this person] be taken to a public place to be hung and strangled until death follows at a gallows erected for this purpose. [It] will be installed in the accustomed place. His body will remain there for 24 hours and will then be exposed near the sea. [The remainder is undecipherable.]
*Decreed and executed in the Council Chamber on 7th July 1730.*

*DUMAS*

On 7 July 1730, whilst being taken to the gallows in Saint-Paul's public square, Le Vasseur threw a cryptogram into the crowd, later found in the Seychelles, and shouted out: "Find my treasure, ye who may understand it!" At five o'clock in the afternoon, on the dot, Le Vasseur was hung "high and short until dead" ("high" so that people could see and "short" so as not to

squander good rope). Le Vasseur's grave is still visible in Saint-Paul, but nobody knows whether it actually contains his body.

## Other Indian Ocean Pirates

Hunted down in the Caribbean by the Royal and Spanish navies, some pirates accepted the amnesty proffered by the English Crown, but many did not. For these diehards, the leading option was to travel to the Indian Ocean. For nearly half a century, from 1685 to 1730, there were about 1,000 pirates, mainly English, American, French and Dutch, prowling the Red Sea, the Persian Gulf, the Malabar Coast and the Indian Ocean.

Here is a non-exhaustive list of these pirates: Adam Baldridge, Andrew Barton, Ned Becker, Jacques Beda, Samuel Bellamy alias Black Sam, Jean Bloqueman, Pierre Boisson, George Booth, François Boucher, Joseph Bradish, Samuel Burgess, Caracioli (Dominican priest), Thomas Cavendish, Louis Chauveau, John Clayton, Thomas Cocklyn, Thomas Collins alias

ABOVE: Poop deck of a 74-gun man-of-war.
*Drawing by L.Garneray, engraved by Manceau, printed by Chardon Jeune & fils, Paris, 19th century.*

Tom Conduit, Robert Culliford, Howell Davis, Guy Dumesnil, Thomas Elgar, Richard Frowd, Arthur Gardiner, François Garnier, François Gauche, Cornelius George, Henri Grimaud, Joseph de Guigné, John Halsey, Thomas Howard, Jacques Huet, Hubert Hugo, Samuel Hyde, Richard John, Adam Johnson, Jon Jovis, James Kelley, James Kelly, William Kidd, Samuel King, Étienne Le Baillif, Joseph Pierre Le Chartier, Laurent Lemoine, Richard Lievins, Marino, Olivier Misson, Christopher Moody, Bernardin Nageon de l'Etang, Jacques Naze, William Noble, George Noel, Nathaniel North, Joseph Pascale, Launey Pellerin, Frederik Philips, Jacques Picard, Jacques Pitou, James Plantain, Guillaume Planter, John Pro, Gilles de Régimont, Jan Retson, Robert Rich, John Richardson, Victor Riverain, Dirk Chivers, John Rivers, Edward Robert, Pieter Robbertz, Claude Ruelle, Jan Pieter Sekeling, Jean Selin, Simon, Sacheus Stockolme, Ralph Stout, Sweet, Robert Tarby, John Taylor, Thomas Tew, Troussailles, Denis Turpin, Alexander Ure, van Laar, Otto Van Tuyl, David Watkin, Thomas White, Gilbert Widman, David Williams...

## The Descendants of the Pirates and Queen Bety

From 1685 onwards, a number of pirates settled on Île Sainte Marie and founded families, sometimes with several wives, polygamy being allowed on the island. During the 1720s, the offspring from these ex-pirates numbered in the thousands and they formed the second-largest ethnic group on the main island. They were called the Zana Malata – meaning "mixed race".

One of these, Ratsimilaho, known to the Europeans as Tom Smilo, was a slave trader. According to historians, he was the son of a pirate, either of the American Thomas Tew, the Englishman Thomas White or the Englishman Thomas Collins. Two things seem certain: his father was a pirate called Thomas and his mother was Queen Antavaratra Rahena.

ABOVE: Malagasy warrior.
*Drawing by Gérôme, taken from* Madagascar et ses Satellites, *19th century.*

OPPOSITE: The doubloon, a Spanish gold coin that was sought after by pirates. Solid silver Spanish coins came in denominations of 2, 4 or 8 real. The 8-real coin is the famous "piece of eight". Solid gold coins came in 4 or 8 escudo denominations. The latter was called a "doubloon". Two 8-real pieces equalled one escudo or one-sixteenth of a doubloon.

Whichever Thomas it was, he took his son to London where Ratsimilaho received a refined education and became an intelligent, audacious and charismatic young man. On the death of his mother, Ratsimilaho took over as head of the Zana Malata community[15], and went off to conquer the Kingdom of Vatomandry, which included Tamatave and Fenerive (two cities in Madagascar). He then crushed the Tsikoa tribes and soon proclaimed himself as King Ramaromanompo. He named his kingdom Betsimisaraka, "those who are inseparable", and to ensure the support of the Sakalava tribe married the daughter of Andriamahatindriarivo, King of Boina.

His influence, at its peak, spread over 370 miles down the east coast of Madagascar. From his marriage with the Sakalava princess, he had a daughter, Bety[16], born in 1735.

When Ratsimilaho died, Bety became Queen of the Kingdom of Betsimisaraka. She married a certain Jean Onésime Filet (a Frenchman from Casteljaloux in France, often referred to as Corporal La Bigorne) and, probably under his influence, she pursued her father's idea of placing her kingdom under the protection of the French East India Company. She asked for the white flag with the *fleur-de-lys* to be flown over Île Sainte Marie, the power centre of her monarchy, and on the coast from Foulpointe to the Bay of Antongil[17].

---

15. Later on, between 1790 and 1820, the descendants of the Zana Malatas, guided by the Antalaotra tribes of northwest Madagascar, organised raids in the Comoros and on the east coast of Africa to supply the Mascarene islands with slaves.

16. Marie Élisabeth Sobobie, better known as Bety or Betia. The ruins of her palace are still visible on Île Sainte-Marie, along with the graves of several pirates including that of Joseph Pierre Le Chartier.

17. Bety reigned from 1750 to 1754, even though she resided on Île de France. Jean Onésime Filet acted as her "prince consort" on Madagascar for 17 years until 1767, when what was left of the kingdom was taken in hand by a nephew of Bety's named Iavy. Iavy's role was essentially limited to the supply of slaves to the Europeans for their colonisation of the Mascarenes.

PAGES 66 & 67: When all was calm with no enemy or prey in sight, or to celebrate a lucrative haul, a pirate captain would allow his men to celebrate, but it would never be long before it degenerated into a wild drinking binge on deck.
*Engraving by H.Smith taken from* L'Univers Illustré, *Michel Lévy frères, Paris, 1859.*

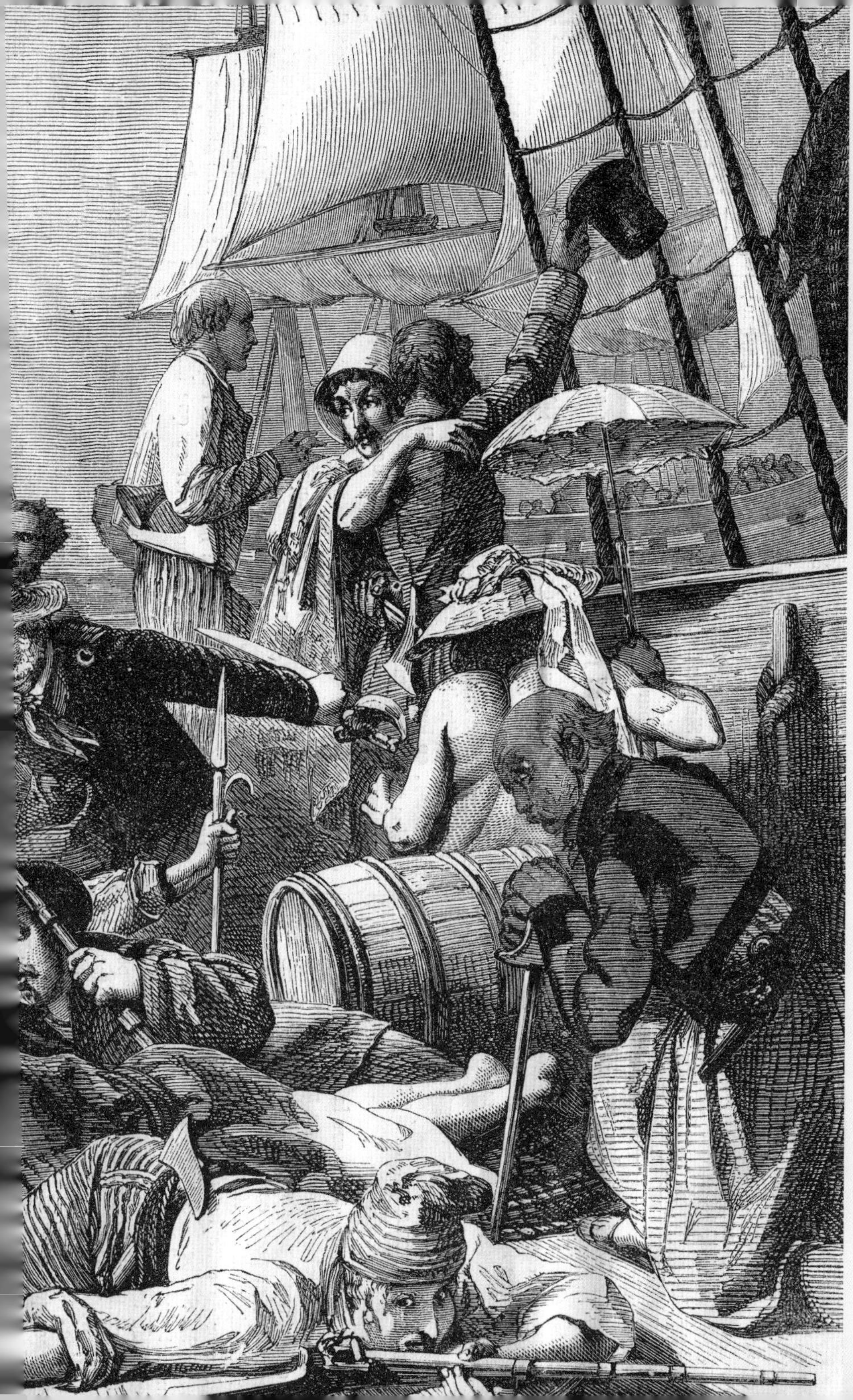

ABOVE: An *Ara macao*, or scarlet macaw, one of the 350 species of parrots belonging to the Psittacidae family. Fables have it that pirates often carried parrots on their shoulders. It is true that tropical parrots have wonderfully extravagant plumage and that they can be good imitators of human speech. More importantly, perhaps, it is said that parrots can predict the weather: the restless and chatty behaviour at night means changeable weather is imminent, while insistent preening indicates storms on the horizon. Nevertheless, Robert Louis Stevenson, author of *Treasure Island*, may well have fathered this legend when he put a parrot on Long John Silver's shoulder.

OPPOSITE: In 1775, Queen Bety was baptised by Father Delfolie in the church of Saint Louis in Port Louis. *19th century engraving.*

On 30 July 1750, this policy received the approbation of around 60 of the local chiefs, in whose presence an agreement was signed at an official ceremony on board the *Mars*, with Adam de Villiers and Guillaume Gosse representing Barthélémy David, the Governor of Île de France and Île Bourbon. The treaty between France and Queen Bety provided for "the complete surrender without any restrictions of Île Sainte Marie, of its port and the islet which encloses it, [...] without having to pay her, Bety, nor any of her successors, any rights or payments for the aforementioned acquisition."

Even though a vast majority was in favour of this handover, it did not please everyone. On 19 September 1750, Betsimisaraka's opponents, led by the Princes Siba and Tsifanda, massacred several French people including Guillaume Gosse, the representative of the French East India Company, who had apparently desecrated Ratsimilaho's grave, the act responsible for triggering the revolt.

In 1751, Queen Bety, accompanied by her mother Mamadion and some of the survivors of the massacre, crossed over to Île de France where, during a meeting of the Superior Council, she had no trouble convincing her audience of her total innocence in the affair. The French authorities then made another attempt at taking possession of Île Sainte Marie in 1753 while Queen Bety was residing on Île de France, where she stayed until 1756. There she was respected by the senior dignitaries of the island's administration, and admired for her great beauty and kindness. After spending some time in Madagascar, she returned in 1762 to calm the smouldering ambitions of her half-brother Jean Hare, also known as Zanhary, who was considerably assuaged when Bety gave him Foulpointe. This was undoubtedly, however, the start of the kingdom's disintegration.

Back on Île de France, Queen Bety acquired several sizeable landholdings in different parts of the island to add to her concession near Port Louis,

which she had owned since 1758. She maintained friendly relations with one of the senior officers of the Île de France garrison, René Charles Le François de Grainville, also known as Forval de Grainville, who also participated in the administration of Île Sainte Marie. Queen Bety, the granddaughter of a pirate, spent her declining years on Île de France between her residence at Vacoas in the Grand-Port area and her house in the neighbourhood of Port Louis. She died in 1805, aged 70.

## Treasure Hunting in Mauritius

For many years, treasure hunters have been swarming to the Mascarenes and the Seychelles to find treasure hidden by the pirates, in some secret places in one of the islands of these archipelagos. However, given that there were about 1,000 pirates on Madagascar from 1685 to 1730, it is not impossible that a treasure, stashed away nearly three centuries ago, is still there.

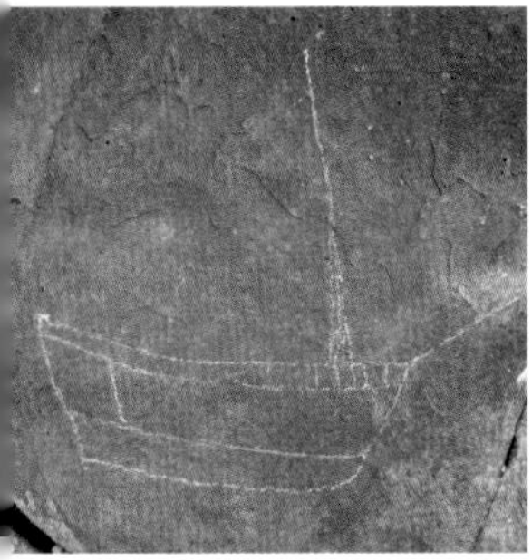

ABOVE: Image of a sailing boat carved into a rock at Belmont, not far from the "jen Bow n e de pacqu" inscription. These carvings were discovered when a sugar company named Saint-Antoine was clearing some land in 1927. (In this photo, the grooves carved into the volcanic rock have been highlighted in chalk to make them more visible.)

OPPOSITE: A Coolie chieftain armed with his sabre and katar, a dagger whose handle is perpendicular to its blade.
*Engraving by T. Wageman,* Oriental Memoirs, *James Forbes, 1834.*

PAGES 72 & 73: A 19th-century French man-of-war during a naval battle.
*Drawing by Antoine Léon Morel-Fatio.*

Pirates captured hundred of ships, and stripped them of their valuables, which were then stored in sturdy iron chests. To prevent them from being stolen, the pirate captain, accompanied only by a few trusted companions, would discreetly bury the precious plunder near the shore of deserted islands. Naturally, the pirate had every intention of returning at some later date to retrieve his hoard, notably to provide for his retirement years. Unforeseen circumstances, however, not lacking in the careers of these sea rogues, meant that these treasure troves were not always recovered.

A good example of this relates to Olivier Le Vasseur. After dividing up the spoils from the *Nossa Senhora do Cabo* in April 1721, Le Vasseur found himself in Madagascar with his share of the loot. From his base in Île Sainte Marie, he continued his career as a pirate in the Indian Ocean until December of the same year, when he decided to call a halt to his plundering and to settle down to a more peaceful life. Nearly ten years later in 1730, on the orders of the governor of Île Bourbon, Le Vasseur was arrested on Île Sainte Marie and taken as a prisoner to Saint-Paul. So, what did he do with his treasure? Everything points to the possibility that most of it, at least, had been hidden in a secret place that only he knew the location of. This hypothesis was reinforced on 7 July 1730, when Le Vasseur threw a mysterious cryptogram supposedly indicating his hoard's hiding place into the crowd which had come to witness his hanging. According to the historian Auguste Toussaint[18], this coded message was later found amongst the documents of the pirate Bernardin Nageon de l'Étang who died in Madagascar in 1795. Le Vasseur's cryptogram has sparked off countless treasure hunts of all manner and size, both on Mauritius and in the Seychelles.

18. Auguste Toussaint, *Dictionnaire de Biographie Mauricienne/Dictionary of Mauritian Biography*, journal No. 12, December 1943, p. 362.

On Mauritius, there have been excavations in the Rivière Noire district, at Klondike in 1902 and 1912; at Walhalla in 1925; and in the Grand Port area at Pointe Vacoas in 1926. The centre of interest then shifted to the site of Belmont near Poudre d'Or where excavations carried out in 1927 unearthed ringbolts, cannonballs, a rock in the shape of a tortoise, and some human bones. In 1932, more excavations were carried out at Petit-Sable, at Pointe Vacoas, then at Klondike and Tamarin in 1940 and 1950. In 1960, the lagoon off Pointe aux Roches was explored by a diviner. Over the years other sites have attracted feverish interest, such as Bel Ombre, La Cambuse, Baie du Tombeau, Petite Rivière and, more recently, Souillac.

To this day, no treasure has been found on Mauritius even though there are visible signs. Near Poudre d'Or, on one of the volcanic rocks which line the shore is a clearly carved ship. On another rock, there is the inscription "jen bow n e de pacqu", barely visible and somewhat mysterious; further along, another rock is carved in the shape of a boot. According to Pierre Maurice[19], an old bottle of rum, some musket balls, another boot-shaped rock and a bit of a pipe were found in an underground gallery at Souillac.

It only takes a few signs to stir up a bit of greed and to inspire generations of treasure hunters. A story was told of a morning in 1860, at dawn on the east coast of Mauritius, when the caretaker of the Grande Retraite dwelling house spotted some men digging close to a small hillock not far from the shoreline. Standing a few metres away, armed men waited beside two small rowing boats. The caretaker ran off to summon his employer. On their return, the suspicious individuals had disappeared. Where the men had been digging was a passage that led to a pit. On the beach were empty caskets and footprints.

19. Pierre Maurice, 'L'île aux trésors', *Islander*, No. 43, Mauritius, April–June 2006.

## PRIVATEERS IN THE INDIAN OCEAN

The terms 'pirate' and 'privateer' are sometimes used interchangeably; however, they refer to quite distinct activities. Privateers were fully licensed by their motherland to operate by and for their country in times of war. Pirates, on the other hand, operated illegally and on their own behalf. This distinction was made in the eyes of the law in France in the 17th century. Famous privateers during the reign of Louis XIV included the Baron of Pointis, Jean Bart, Count Claude de Forbin and René Duguay-Trouin, who between them succeeded in capturing several hundred ships from the English.

During the American War of Independence (1778–1783), while Louis XVI's soldiers led by Lafayette and Rochambeau supported General Washington's troops against the English, the government in Versailles officially authorised the arming of ships for privateering. The French authorities delivered 'letters of marque' or 'letters of reprisal' to shipowners as well as to private individuals, according them official license to act as combatants. Privateer boats were essentially merchant ships that had been equipped for battle.

The Pitot de la Beaujardière brothers, close relatives of Robert Surcouf, were the first shipowners in Île de France to partake in this adventure. Their vessel, *Philippine*, set sail from Port Louis on 17 April 1780 under the command of Captain Claude Deschiens de Kérulvay (nicknamed Furious

Dog by the English), who was 35 at the time. Starter's orders had been given: the privateers' war in the Indian Ocean was underway.

At the time, the Admiralty of the French Navy was largely made up of members of the aristocracy. During the period of the French Revolutionary and Napoleonic Wars (1792–1815), a number of admirals were eliminated, while others fled the guillotine, some even going to live abroad. This left the French Navy in chaos, and with no choice but to depend even more on privateers in the fight against Britain's all-powerful Royal Navy. There were over 100 privateers based in Île de France at this time, charged with weakening Great Britain by attacking the vessels of the East India Company, which operated the lucrative trade with India, the East and the Far East that underpinned England's economy and military power.

For privateers, Île de France offered major advantages, not least of which was its port (Port Louis), which was considerably better equipped than Île Bourbon's Saint-Denis, whose facilities were appalling. Settlers on both islands suffered from a lack of supplies, as their harvests were regularly destroyed by cyclones, leaving them unable to feed their populations. Blockades imposed by the Royal Navy in the area only served to make things worse. French privateers who made a series of prizes and brought the

PAGE 74: Robert Surcouf, aged 23, aboard the *Hasard* and preparing his crew of 19 men to board the *Triton*, an East Indiaman armed with 26 cannons, in the Bay of Bengal in 1796.
*Drawing by Alfred Paris, 19th-century engraving.*

PAGE 75 (TOP): Jean Bart (1650–1702), a French privateer of Flemish origin, took 50 prizes between 1674 and 1678. He captained a frigate under Louis XIV in 1679, fighting the Barbary corsairs in the Mediterranean, and ended his career as squadron Commodore.

PAGE 75 (BOTTOM): René Duguay-Trouin (1673–1736), a privateer from St Malo active from 1689 to 1697 under Louis XIV, captured 16 enemy men-of-war and approximately 300 merchant ships. In 1711, at the head of a flotilla of 15 ships, he took Rio de Janeiro, which at the time was under Portuguese rule. He ended his career as a Lieutenant General in the Navy.

## Privateers' vessels

Privateers' boats were smaller, faster and more manoeuvrable than the East India Company's imposing vessels. Some of them weighed less than 100 tons, and were equipped with just a few cannons and 30 or so sailors. Others, however, like *La Psyché* (a corsair built in Nantes in 1797 and commanded by Captain Léveillé) were as large as 600 tons, with 34 cannons and a crew of 278 men – out-and-out weapons of mass destruction for the period.

The crews were a motley bunch, including Malays, lascars (a Persian word for Indian sailors), Kaffirs (here referring a Bantu ethnic group), prisoners of different nationalities and, more rarely, deserters from the French Navy. Emancipated slaves were also frequently found on board.

J. Milbert del. et sc. Pyeot sc.

Île-de-France.

*Porte d'entrée de la ville du Port Napoléon.*

captured foodstuffs back to shore were therefore welcomed with open arms by the local population. Inventories were made of the ships and goods taken from the English, which were then sold at public auctions. A Council of Prizes was established in Port Louis to handle these cases and oversee the division of spoils between the French State, the shipowners and the crews. An invalids' fund was created to cover the needs of the wounded or the families of sailors who had been killed in combat.

Two privateers in particular stood out for their exploits: Robert Surcouf, nicknamed 'the king of privateers', originally from St Malo, and Jacques Perroud, originally from Bordeaux. Together with Nicolas Surcouf, Robert's brother, they were the only privateers to receive the Legion of Honour under Napoleon. English vessels were frequently captured thanks to incessant raids by privateers roaming the Southern Seas, who were ready to fight to the

ABOVE: In 1806, in order to attract Napoleon's attention to the Île de France's precarious situation, Governor Decaen renamed Port-Nord-Ouest (presently Port Louis) to 'Port-Napoleon'.

*Drawing by J. Milbert, engraved by Pyeot, taken from the atlas of* Voyage pittoresque à l'île de France, au cap de Bonne-Espérance et à l'île de Ténériffe, *J. Milbert, Paris, 1812.*

OPPOSITE: Napoleon dressed in his famous uniform of Colonel of the Imperial Guard's Chasseurs à Cheval (the light cavalry that provided the Emperor with a personal escort). In 1803, Napoleon invited Robert Surcouf to the chateau of Saint-Cloud where he offered him the rank of ship's captain in command of a flotilla. Wishing to retain his independence, Surcouf boldly set conditions to his acceptance, causing Napoleon to retract his offer.

*Drawing by Isabey, engraved by Langlois, 19th century.*

The Church of Pamplemousses (1756), made famous by Bernardin de Saint-Pierre's novel *Paul et Virginie*. Its cemetery holds the tombs of many people who marked the island's history during the 18th and 19th centuries. The St Malo privateer Jean Marie Dumaine de la Josserie, captain in the merchant navy and comrade-in-arms to Robert Surcouf, is buried here, having died in Port Louis in 1846.

*Drawing by Paris, engraved by Himely, taken from* Voyage autour du monde par les mers de l'Inde et de la Chine de la corvette de sa Majeste *La Favorite* exécuté pendant les annees 1830, 1831, 1832 sous le commandement de M. Laplace..., *Imprimerie royale, Paris, 1835.*

death for their homeland, honour... and money. Between 1807 and 1809, 14 vessels belonging to the East India Company were captured by French privateers; the bounty was in excess of US$6 million.[20] Robert Surcouf's great-great-nephew provided detailed figures for the prizes on both sides during the period 1793 to 1797: the French captured 2,226 vessels belonging to the English and their allies, while the English managed just 375 French prizes.[21] This vast difference in favour of the French gives some idea of the constant raids to which English trade was subject, and explains the famous statement of Lord Chatham: "While the French hold Île de France, the English will never be masters of the Indies."

This situation was not only humiliating for Great Britain but also financially ruinous. The decision was therefore taken to strike at the heart of the problem. On 2 December 1810, English naval troops landed in force on Île de France, overwhelming the island's military forces and obliging its French governor, General Decaen, to sign the act of surrender. Henceforth the island fell under British rule and took back its Dutch name, Mauritius. This sudden change of sovereignty brought the privateers' domination of the Indian Ocean during the Republican and Imperial eras to a definitive end.

It was not until 1856, however, that privateering was officially abolished at the Congress of Paris. The United States, Spain and Mexico did not sign the treaty.

**TOP:** Captain Duperré was in command of the *Bellone* during the battle of Grand Port in August 1810 – this French naval victory is depicted on the pediment of the Arc de Triomphe in Paris. *19th-century lithograph.*

**BOTTOM:** Captain Willoughby, in command of the frigate *Néréide* during the Battle of Grand Port, received a serious injury to his eye. *Painting by Thomas Barber, c 1830.*

## François Yves Carosin (1762–1794)

François Yves Carosin was born on 22 February 1762 in Saint-Énogat (now

20. Philippe Lenoir, *Île Maurice, ancienne île de France*, Éditions du Cygne, Mauritius, 1979.
21. Robert Surcouf, *Un capitaine corsaire, Robert Surcouf*, Plon, Paris, 1925.

## Claude Beguin Matelot

Labrousse, del. sculp.

*Les lâches trahissent leur patrie,*
*Les hommes généreux meurent pour elle.*

15, Fructidor, An. Ier

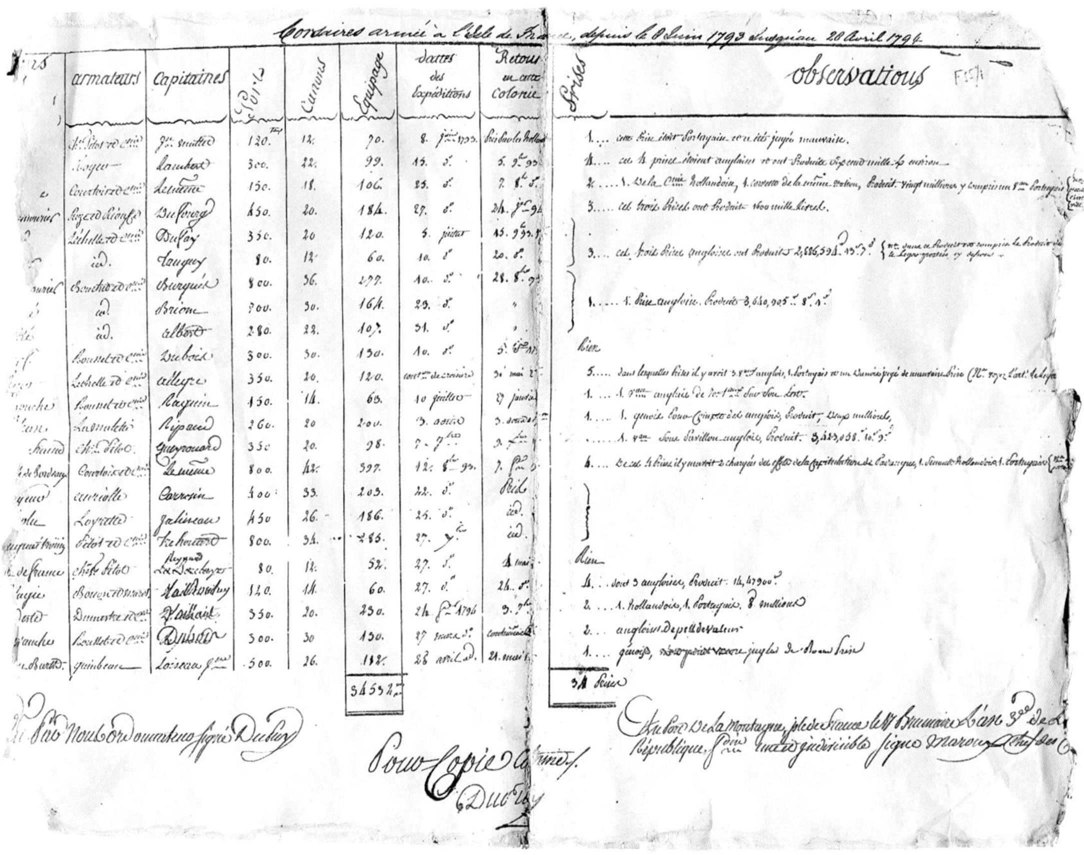
Corsaires armés à l'Isle de France, depuis le 8 Juin 1793 jusqu'au 28 Avril 1794

| armateurs | Capitaines | Port | Canons | Equipage | dattes des expéditions | Retour en cette Colonie | Prises | observations |
|---|---|---|---|---|---|---|---|---|

Dinard). He was the fourth of five sons of Françoise Jeanne Piet and Augustin François Carosin, a captain in France's merchant navy.

During his youth in Saint-Énogat, he saved a man from drowning, but in the process was badly wounded on his face, the scar of which he bore for the rest of his life. In 1779 he was chief mate aboard a small vessel named the *Rusée*. He then served successively as assistant pilot on the *Triton* and the *Amphion*, before taking up command of the *Marguerite* in March 1781. This

**ABOVE:** Document listing the numerous prizes taken by the privateers of Île de France over a 10-month period (June 1793–April 1794).

**PAGE 81:** The Battle of Grand Port, with the scuttling of HMS *Sirius* in the foreground.
*After a painting by Pierre-Julien Gilbert, engraved by Chavane, diagraphed and pantographed by Gavard, 19th century.*

ABOVE (LEFT): On the right, a boarding cutlass known as a 'cuillère à pot' (lit. 'pot spoon') and, on the left, a 'briquet' sabre typical of the Napoleonic infantry, but also used for boarding.

ABOVE (RIGHT): While anchored in the port of Mahé in the Seychelles to offload 32 deportees suspected of having plotted against Napoleon, the 36-cannon frigate *Chiffone* was captured by the 38-cannon English frigate HMS *Sybille*. The French ship suffered 23 deaths and 30 wounded.
*English print engraved by Sutherland.*

PAGE 82: During the French revolutionary wars, patriotism intensified, spurring citizens to act like heroes, as the sailor Claude Beguin is seen doing here. The behaviour of the privateer François Carosin in 1794 is an outstanding example of the heroism and patriotism of the period.
*Drawing and engraving by Labrousse, 1793.*

was short-lived, for by the following year he was second-in-command on board the *Actif* captained by Hasiette, and by 1783, he was ship's lieutenant on the *Andromaque*, then second-in-command under Augustin Carosin, his brother, on the *Aimable Perette*.

In 1785, he sailed to the East Indies on the *Martinique*. Not long after he returned home in St Malo in May 1786, he was given command of the *Alexandre*, bound for Île de France. His younger brother, Mathurin Carosin, was the vessel's second lieutenant. Marthe Blanc, the daughter of the former French Consul in Saint-Jean-d'Acre, was also on board.[22]

In November 1786, a few months after his arrival in Île de France, François Yves Carosin married Marie Louise de La Haye Duponsel. Having

22. Daughter of Zacharie Blanc, Marthe Blanc married Antoine Jean Caïez d'Épinay, a lawyer at the Parlement de Paris and in Île de France, who later became a member of the Assemblée Coloniale. She was mother to the lawyer and politician Adrien d'Épinay and future grandmother of the sculptor Prosper d'Épinay.

settled in Moka, he was appointed a member of the Assemblée Coloniale (the seat of the colonial government), and then municipal prosecutor for the Moka district in 1792. By the time he set sail in pursuit of English ships in October 1793, he was father to two daughters and in command of the frigate *Vengeur*, which he and a certain Auriolle had equipped for privateering. Just days before the birth of his third child, François Carosin captured four enemy vessels in succession. Encouraged by this success, he set sail for the Sunda Islands, a popular port of call for English vessels.

As he approached Sumatra, François Carosin noticed an East India Company vessel that was armed for battle. He ordered all hands to action stations. With cannons roaring on both sides, he was about to give the command to board when an English cannonball ripped through him, severing both his legs in an instant. Undaunted, the still-conscious Carosin bravely asked his men to place him upright in a barrel filled with cinders

LEFT: Rue Desforges (now Sir Seewoosagur Ramgoolam Street) in Port Louis.

*Drawing by Alfred Erny, engraved by Hotelin Hurel, taken from* Le Tour du Monde, *Librairie L. Hachette et Cie, Paris, 1863.*

PAGES 86 & 87: "Everybody is at his post. The two ships board each other. It's general action stations and the attack is sounded on the drum. [...] The enemy is faced by sailors full of enthusiasm who, with lips pursed in anger and bloodshot eyes, prepare to throw themselves like tigers onto them. [...] The combat ceases to be combat and becomes an almighty carnage. [...] The fight is no longer human; people tear each other apart, bite each other, slit each other's throats."

*Freely translated from Louis Garneray's description of the boarding of the* Kent *by Surcouf and his crew.*

and sand, from which he was able to give the command to board the enemy ship. However, the firepower of the English ship proved superior and François Carosin could only watch helplessly as the *Vengeur* was destroyed. His men were progressively decimated by the enemy fire; soon only his number two, Desveaux, and one other sailor remained at his side. In a burst of pride, no doubt sparked by anger at having lost his legs, François Carosin asked to be brought the French flag. He placed it between his teeth and attempted to throw himself into the sea to avoid being taken captive, preferring to die alongside his country's colours. The English, however, were already aboard the frigate and one of His Majesty's officers grabbed hold of him. François Carosin was brought on board the enemy ship where he died soon after, despite the careful assistance provided by the English. Today, there are still many descendents of Augustin Carosin, François' elder brother, living in Mauritius.

ABOVE: View of St Malo – the starting point for numerous expeditions to the New World in the 16th century.

*Drawing by L. Garneray, engraved by P. Brunellière, Paris, 19th century.*

OPPOSITE: Portrait of the privateer François Le Même (postage stamp issued in 1972). After he was set free in 1802, he settled in Île de France as a trader and banker.

## François Thomas Le Même (1764–1805)

François Thomas Le Même was born in St Malo on 13 January 1764, son of Jacques Henri Le Même and Gertrude Bodin. Navigating fascinated him from an early age, and he persuaded his parents to allow him to take classes in hydrography.

In 1778, Le Même was hired as a volunteer on a merchant ship bound for North America. It was the start of the American War of Independence, and he found himself with Captain Boynard on board the *Prince de Montbarrey*. The ship was captured by the English, and the 15-year-old François was taken prisoner. A year later he was liberated as part of an exchange, probably for some English prisoners.

He pursued a career with the French Navy until 1783, then sailed with merchant ships in order to improve his navigational skills. By January 1790, he had reached the rank of captain, and the following year he was put in charge of the *Liberté*, a three-master bound for Île de France.

He sailed into the harbour of Port Louis for the first time in December 1791. He then continued on to Pondicherry and Bengal, before returning to Île de France. Thereafter, in command of the *Hirondelle,* he sailed to the Dutch East Indies (present-day Indonesia) , where he spent 10 months on a mission before returning yet again to Île de France.

In June 1793, war was declared between England and France. Captain Le Même armed the *Hirondelle* for privateering, leaving the harbour of Port Louis on 10 June in search of enemy ships. He encountered two English ships in quick succession, both of which he successfully attacked, captured and brought back to Île de France. Spurred by these victories, Le Même made a further five forays in command of, successively, the *Ville de Bordeaux*, the *Amphytrite*, the *Uni*, the *Clarisse* and the *Grande Hirondelle*, each time returning to Port Louis with ample bounty. Thanks to his daring and navigational skills, it did not take Le Même long to acquire a tidy fortune. During a foray in 1801, however, he was captured by an English vessel, the HMS *Sybille*, and taken prisoner. He was not freed until the following year, with the signing of the Treaty of Amiens.

Upon his liberation, Le Même decided to try his hand at trading and banking in Île de France. He did not, however, prove to be good at either, and his fortune dwindled rapidly. With the renewed outbreak of hostilities between England and France in 1803, Le Même was one of the first to gear up for privateering, in command of his boat *La Fortune*.

He returned to Île de France in May 1804 at the head of a convoy of eight captured English vessels, and was greeted by an eager throng lining the quays of Port Louis' harbour. Surcouf himself could not have done better. By August, Le Même was off again on a new campaign. He soon encountered a powerful East Indiaman, the *Concord*, off the coast of India. He could not resist and launched an attack, but his daring got the better of him. Despite putting up a bitter struggle, he and his crew failed to gain the upper hand, and their ship was captured on 7 November. Le Même was taken to Bombay and imprisoned there.

The English authorities decided to send him to England, and put him on board a Royal Navy ship, the *Walterston*, that weighed anchor from the port of Bombay on 15 February 1805. The privateer Le Même died at sea during the voyage aged 41.

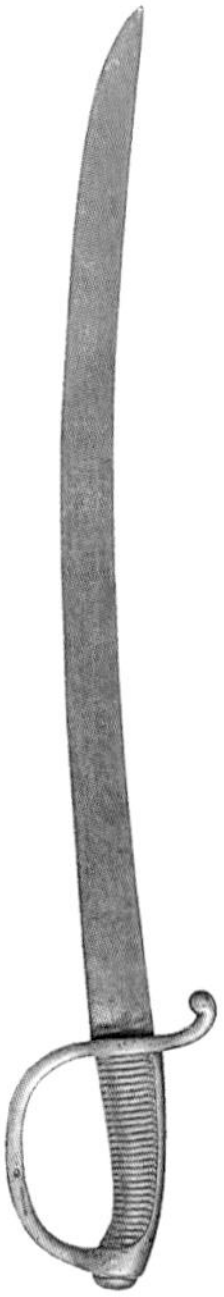

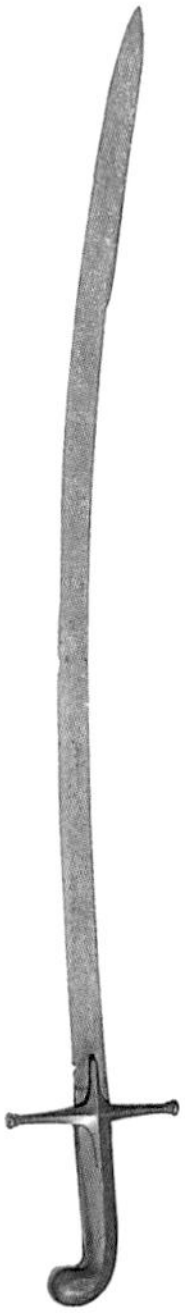

ABOVE (LEFT): According to the National History Museum in Mahébourg, this sabre belonged to the privateer Joachim Drieu. After the surrender of the *Kent*, Joachim Drieu made a triumphant entry into Port Louis at its helm in October 1800, having been put in command of it by Surcouf.
*National History Museum, Mahébourg.*

ABOVE (RIGHT): According to the National History Museum in Mahébourg, this sabre belonged to Captain Rivington, Commander of the *Kent*, and was given to Surcouf after the ship's surrender.
*National History Museum, Mahébourg.*

## Joachim Marie Drieu (1767–1835)

Joachim Marie Drieu, son of François Drieu and Marie Nepveu, was born in St Malo in 1767, and began work in the merchant navy at a very young age.

His first visit to Île de France in February 1777 was as a mere ship's boy aboard the *Père de Famille*, a ship commanded by his father. 13 years later,

he was appointed a captain fit for long haul voyages in Port Louis, and took command of the *Citoyen Français*. He subsequently explored the coast of Madagascar aboard the *Julien* and, in 1794, during the French revolutionary wars, he set sail from Port Louis as second-in-command to Captain Levaillant aboard the *Modeste*.

In August 1796, at the age of 29, he was given a mission by Rear Admiral Marquis de Sercey, captain of the French Navy in the Indian Ocean at that time. Joachim Drieu's ostensible task was to locate an English squadron, but the Rear Admiral's real purpose was to attack the island of Penang, off the west coast of the Malay Peninsula.

Captain Joachim Drieu, in charge of the *Alerte* and armed with a letter of marque, flushed out an English ship, the *Carysfort*, off the coast from Negapatam. He attacked it, thinking it was a merchant ship. By the time he

Landing stage in Pondicherry. The privateer Drieu, in command of the *Alerte*, suffered a resounding defeat at the hands of a powerful English vessel in 1796, off the coast of Negapatam. He was imprisoned in Pondicherry, where he remained for two years.
*Drawing by M. de Sainson,* Voyage autour du monde, *Jules Dumont-d'Urville, Paris, 1834.*

INDE
LAURISTON, NÉ A PONDICHÉRY en 1768
ARMES DE FRANCE
Myriamètres
INDOUSTAN
DEKHAN
MER D'OMAN
MER DES INDES
GOLFE DU BENGALE
CUZERATE
ORISSA
CÔTE DE MALABAR
CÔTE DE COROMANDEL
CEYLAN
ILES LAKEDIVES
ILES MALDIVES
Odeypour
Rin
Bhoudj
G. de Kutch
Cambaye
Barode
Pourbender
Surate
Bombay
Poonah
Goa
Ghériah
Mangalore
Seringapatam
Mahé
Calicut
Cochin
Trivanderam
C. Comorin
Banc Padua
I. Aménè
I. Seuhélipar
I. Underout
I. Kalpeni
I. Minicoy
OUDJEIN
Canroudy
Nagpour
Ellichpour
Aureng-abad
Nandair
Sirpour
Bamghir
Golconde
Hayderabad
Solapour
Beyjajapour
Guntour
Yanaon
Madapollam
Mazulipatam
Kistnah R.
Kurnoul
Angole
Nellore
Tripatty
MADRAS
Sadras
PONDICHÉRY
Tranquebar
Karikal
Tanjore
Madura
Tondi
Tuticorin
Salem
Combatour
G. de Manaar
Colombo
Pte de Galle
Pic d'Adam
Hambantotte
Batticala
Trinquemale
Puttam
Sombelpour
Sohnpour
Bamragour
Patnaa
Kétek
Balasore
Bastar
Chicacole
Visagapatam
Bandour
Ganjam
Rondy
Jellasore
Chandernagor
Serampour
CALCUTTA
Hougly
Dacca
Luckipour
Islamabad
Bouches du Gange
Rottunpour
Patcoum
Jaipour
Bauranpour
Baroda
Ile et Fᵗ Diu
C. de Cambaye
Meritch
Adoni
Darwar
Sounda
Mysour
Arcot
Gingée
Devicotta
Cananor
Cotiote
Pt de Palk
Maison du Port de Pondichéry.
Eléphant Caparaçonné.

realised he was up against a sloop-of-war, it was too late. The situation quickly turned to his disadvantage, and the *Alerte* was captured by the English. Drieu was taken prisoner and transported to Pondicherry.

It was two years before he was released, in 1798, at which point he returned to Île de France.

At the start of the following year, he requested another letter of marque. This required him to explain why he had attacked the *Carysfort*, a mistake to all intents and purposes. When the *Alerte* had been captured, the Marquis de Sercey's instructions had fallen into the hands of the English, and the Rear Admiral was forced to abandon his project for attacking Penang. Drieu's explanation failed to convince the governor, Hippolyte de Maurès, Count of Malartic, and his request was rejected. This left Joachim Drieu unable to command a privateer's vessel.

A few months later, however, Drieu got lucky: Robert Surcouf was in the port and preparing to embark upon a campaign. Drieu succeeded in convincing Surcouf to enrol him, and he soon found himself as second-in-command on board the *Confiance*.

In May 1800, the *Confiance* left Port Louis for a campaign in the Indian Ocean. On 7 October 1800, after many months of navigating, it crossed paths with the *Kent*, a vast and majestic 1200-tonner East Indiaman armed with 38 large-calibre cannons and carrying over 400 soldiers.

Captain Surcouf launched an attack, and soon captured the vessel. On board the *Kent*, the second-in-command and the crew surrendered; their captain, Robert Rivington, had been killed by a grenade thrown from the crow's nest by a sailor named Avriot.

Joachim Drieu, who had taken an active part in this attack, was named captain of the captured ship by Surcouf, who conferred him with the honour of sailing it back to Port Louis. On 18 November 1800, Drieu made

OPPOSITE: Map of India from the 19th century, showing the former French trading posts along the Coromandel coast and Mahé on the Malabar coast.

*Map drawn up by the geographer A. Vuillemin, engraved by Ch. Dyonnet. Views by Alès, éditeur-libraire J. Migeon, Paris, 1869.*

PAGES 94 & 95: Boarding and capture of the *Kent* by Robert Surcouf and the crew of the *Confiance* on 7 October 1800 in the Bay of Bengal.

*Drawn and engraved by Morel Fatio, after a painting by Louis Garneray.*

**ABOVE:** An old 12-pound carronade.
*Drawing by Cook, engraved by Rouargue Jeune, 19th century.*

**OPPOSITE:** A naval officer laying down his weapons after his ship is boarded by privateers.
*Drawn and engraved by Rouargue Jeune, printer Chardon Jeune et fils, Paris, 19th century.*

**PAGES 98 & 99:** The interior of a frigate's battery.
*Drawing by L. Garneray, engraved by Manceau, 19th century.*

a triumphal entry into the port of the small French colony in command of the *Kent*, the pride of the East India Company.

In October 1801, Joachim Drieu married Françoise Richard, settling down to a quiet life on Île de France with his three children, a son and two daughters. He died in the Rivière du Rempart district at the age of 68 in 1835, leaving behind a ship's log from the *Confiance*, which has since found its way to the Musée National de la Marine in Paris.[23] Captain Rivington's sword, which Captain Drieu had appropriated, was subsequently returned to the British. Drieu still has numerous descendants in Mauritius today, including the journalist-writer Jean-Pierre Lenoir.

## Jacques François Perroud (1770–1822)

Jacques Perroud was born on 13 November 1770 in Bordeaux, a city with a rich maritime history. At the age of 19 he made his first trip to Île de France aboard the *Aimable Rosalie* as an apprentice in the merchant navy. He returned to Bordeaux and then set sail again for Île de France in January 1792. He then served as second lieutenant on the *Aimable Lucie*, which made its way to India before returning to Île de France in June 1793.

His next post took him up a rank to lieutenant aboard the corsair *Résolu*, which was soon obliged to return to port for repairs. No sooner had Perroud

23. The authorship of this logbook is disputed: while Marcelle Lagesse believes that it was written by Joachim Drieu, Charles Cunat is of the opinion that the privateer Jean Marie Dumaine de la Josserie was its author (Marcelle Lagesse, *Ces hommes de la mer*, Éditions IPC, Mauritius, 1994; and Charles Cunat, *Robert Surcouf*, La Découvrance, Rennes, 1994).

arrived that he signed up with the *Léger*, fitted out by the merchants Louis Léchelle and François Robert and bound for the Persian Gulf, the west coast of India and the Sunda Islands. Back in Île de France, he served first on the *Phoenix* and then on the *Pélagie*. In 1796, he embarked the corsair *Entreprise*, under Captain François Legars. Their first encounter with the enemy resulted in the capture of the English galley *Hay*, a vessel ideal for privateering. Captain Legars put Perroud in charge of it, under whose command it was renamed *Général Pichegru*. Now a captain, Jacques Perroud took a series of prizes: the *Kaunitz*, the *Lark*, the *Castor* and the *Peggi*, of which the first three were brought back to Île de France, while the fourth was sunk by Perroud.[24] On 10 March 1797, Jacques Perroud proudly entered the harbour of Port Louis in command of the *Hay*.

Two years later, Perroud was appointed captain of the corsair *Hasard*, fitted out by the merchant Pierre Michel Desselière, and received instructions from Governor Malartic to convey some dispatches to Vice Admiral de Sercey off the coast of Java. Having accomplished this task, he crossed paths with an American boat, the *Aurora*, and found himself under attack. Thanks to his cunning and skill, he soon gained the upper hand and captured the American vessel, which he immediately sent to Île de France. In mid-July

24. Octave Béchet, *Dictionnaire de biographie mauricienne*, Bulletin No. 29, 1967, p. 863.

1799, Captain Perroud was himself on the way back to Île de France when he encountered another American ship, the *Russell*, which he proceeded to capture. Taking command of it, he sailed back to Île de France, arriving in September 1799. The following month he made a return trip to Lorient aboard the *Aurora*.

In April 1801 he commanded the corsair *Bellone* and sailed towards Sumatra, Bengal and the east coast of India. The vessels captured during this campaign – the *Amboina*, the *Porcher*, the *Tay*, the *Saleh*, the *John*, the *Traveed*, the *Mage*, the *Pedro* and the *Farquhar* – were all taken to Port Louis. The latter was a particularly interesting haul, laden with rice, sugar, muslin,

SERCEY.

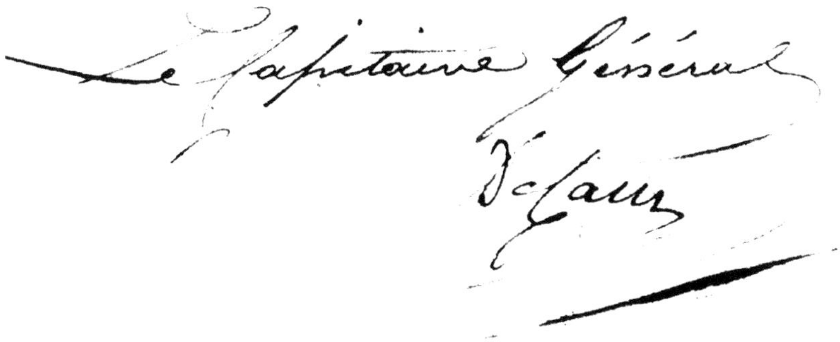

saltpetre, indigo, cotton and wines from Madeira – the wherewithal to delight Île de France's settlers, blighted as they were by food shortages.

Spurred on by this success, Captain Perroud quickly set off again, this time to Europe. In June 1803, he sailed towards the English Channel in command of the *Bellone* and took 10 English prizes off the coast of Ireland, including the *Diamond*, the *Lord Nelson*[25], the *Sophia* and the *Dunkan*.

After all these victories, Jacques Perroud was awarded the Legion of Honour by Napoleon, as well as the 'Hache d'abordage d'honneur' (literally 'boarding axe of honour'), a decoration given by the First Consul to a very limited number of sailors.

By the end of 1804, having spent some time in Bordeaux, Jacques Perroud set sail for Île de France aboard the *Bellone*, with Governor's Decaen's brother-in-law and aide-de-camp, Laurent Bichon de Barrois, as a passenger. During the course of the journey to the small French colony, Perroud added three more vessels to his record: the *Lear*, equipped with 16 cannons; the *Goldstroëm*, a 300-tonner; and the *Henry*.

In October 1805, he quit the harbour of Port Louis aboard the *Bellone*, and headed for the East Indies. This was yet another fruitful campaign that

25. A powerful East Indiaman that Perroud and his crew captured on 14 August 1803 after a particularly harsh boarding that lasted several hours.

ABOVE: Signature of Governor Charles Decaen (1769–1832). He oversaw the lengthy negotiations with the English in December 1810, prior to signing the act of surrender.

OPPOSITE: Vice Admiral Marquis de Sercey (1753–1836), Commander-in-Chief of the French naval forces based in Île de France from 1796 to 1802.

ABOVE: Captain General Charles Decaen, the last French governor of Île Maurice (1803–1810). Postage stamp issued in 2006 to celebrate the 200th anniversary of the town of Mahébourg.

OPPOSITE: View of Government House in the 19th century, giving some idea of the surroundings of the Republic's privateers in the Île de France.
*Lithograph by P. Benoist, printed by Thierry Frères, Paris.*

brought a further seven enemy vessels back to port, including the *Grove*, the *James*, the *Endeavour*, the *Melville* and the *Princess of Wales*. When Perroud himself returned to Île de France in January 1806, however, he had fallen ill and was forced to convalesce onshore.

By November 1807 he was off campaigning again, this time aboard the brig the *Curieux*, travelling to the Sunda Islands, then along the Malayan coast, and even venturing into the China Seas. He was almost certainly the only French privateer to wander into these waters. He made a final stopover in Manila, in the Philippines, before sailing to Île de France where he arrived in May 1809 after another series of attacks and boardings in which he captured the *Marguerite*, the *Amiral Rainier*, the *Betsy* and the *Bradapoo*.

In November of that same year, he took up arms again in command of the *Confiance*, and set sail for France, yet again accompanied by Laurent Bichon de Barrois, this time as General Decaen's emissary to Napoleon to ask for military aid.[26] In February 1810, as they approached the French coast near the Île d'Yeu, the *Confiance* was captured by the *Valiant*, an English vessel. Jacques Perroud was freed, no doubt having given his word that he would no longer take up arms against his captors, or perhaps as a result of exchanging prisoners between France and England, and he took up residence in France. He was soon back in action as a privateer. He was put in command of the *Phoenix* and in June 1810 he was off campaigning in the North Sea, where he successfully took the *Unity* and the *Agenoria*. He then crossed paths with the British vessel the *Eagle* and, for only the second time in 30 years of navigation, he lost and his boat was captured. He was imprisoned by the English for 17 months before being freed and was returned to France.

26. The Île de France was blockaded by the English and the threat of attack was becoming ever more menacing. Governor Decaen was well aware of the imminent danger this represented if reinforcement was not sent quickly by France.

In 1815, shortly after the Treaty of Paris, he made two commercial trips to the Caribbean as captain of the *Joséphine*. He was awarded a diploma to operate as a captain on long-haul trips in 1819, and died not long after in 1822, either in his hometown of Bordeaux, or at sea aboard the *Trois Frères*, depending on which version of the story one believes.[27]

## Jean Marie Dutertre (1770–1811)

Jean Marie Dutertre, who was born in Lorient sometime around 1770, found himself in the Mascarenes when the French Revolution broke out. In 1793, at the age of 23, he was engaged as first lieutenant on board the *Volcan de Mascarin*, a vessel fitted out in Saint-Paul (Réunion) by François Ripaud de Montaudevert, a privateer originally from Brittany.

27. Marcelle Lagesse, *Ces hommes de la mer*, Éditions IPC, Mauritius, 1994.

In July 1798, he took up his first command, setting sail from Port Louis as captain of the *Heureux*. Back in Île de France, he undertook a series of successful campaigns in quick succession, in command of the *Cartier*, the *Modest*, the *Heureux*, the *Passe-Partout*, the *Bonne Cuisine* and, lastly, the *Malartic*. These successes and the bounty won soon earned Dutertre a reputation equal to that of the privateer Robert Surcouf.[28] The first encounter between these two men took place on 19 December 1799, when Dutertre was in command of the *Malartic* and Surcouf of the *Clarisse*. In conversation, each insisted that he had the best crew and

28. Among the objects seized on board one of his prizes, there was a theodolite, an instrument used for making maps and charts. Dutertre sent it to its owner with his "complements in the name of science". This instrument was later used to measure the height of Everest.

chef, and the two of them parted on hostile terms. Not long after, they found themselves together on Île de France, where the situation worsened to a point where they challenged each other to a duel. The governor, the Count of Malartic, hurried to the duel's venue as soon as he got wind of it and, employing all his diplomatic skill, succeeded in reconciling the two men.

Captain Dutertre was captured by the English during a campaign in 1801, and taken prisoner in London, where he remained until after the Treaty of Amiens was signed the following year. By 1803, he was back in Île de France and, as soon as hostilities broke out again between France and England, he lost no time in re-embarking upon campaigns, notably aboard the *Gobe-Mouches*.

Later that year, Governor Decaen charged Dutertre with a delicate mission, that of discretely transporting Courson de la Villeneuve, one of the governor's emissaries, aboard the *Passe-Partout* to a destination on the west coast of India between Goa and Bombay. En route, however, the ship was attacked by the British, and Captain Dutertre was wounded and captured. He was put on board a British vessel bound for England. During a stopover in Île Sainte-Hélène (Saint Helena island), Dutertre managed to slip through the hands of his gaolers and swim out to an American boat anchored in the port and so escaped.

In 1804, he was back in Île de France, this time serving in the Navy. Two years later, he served under Captain Épron as lieutenant aboard the *Piémontaise*, playing an active part in winning the vessel's numerous prizes.

General Decaen recommended Captain Dutertre for the Legion of Honour, but Napoleon's Naval Minister Denis Decrès objected, thus ruining the captain's chance of being decorated.[29] He therefore ended his career as ship's lieutenant, and died in 1811.

29. Marcelle Lagesse, *Ces hommes de la mer*, Éditions IPC, Mauritius, 1994.

ABOVE: Robert Surcouf, the 'king of privateers'. He captured over 47 English vessels. Surcouf made Île de France his base on four separate occasions, spending a total of nine years on the island.

*Postage stamp issued in 1951, drawn and engraved by Charles Mazelin, after a painting by Gustave Alaux, 20th century.*

OPPOSITE (TOP): The Port of St Malo, view from Saint-Servan, opposite the Éperon.

*Engraving by N. Ozanne, naval engineer, 1776.*

OPPOSITE (BOTTOM): Vice Admiral Decrès. He was Napoleon's Naval Minister for 13 years until 1814. He opposed awarding Captain Dutertre with the Legion of Honour.

*Engraving after L. Lauta, 19th century.*

Le Port-Louis, vu du large.

### Robert Surcouf (1773–1827)

France's best-known privateer was born in St Malo on 12 December 1773. By the age of 14, he was a ship's boy aboard the *Héron*. Two years later, he was bound for the East Indies on board the *Aurore* under Captain Tardivet, and made a stopover in Île de France in June 1789. He lived there for the next five years, during which time he served on several ships traversing the Indian Ocean, dealing in slavery for a while in Madagascar and along the East African coast in spite of his country's agreement to abolish slavery.

He was 21 when he was first put in command of a ship, the *Créole*, a brig bearing slaves that was equipped with four cannons and a crew of 30. Then, armed with a clearance certificate[30], he embarked upon privateering in command of the *Emilie*. He returned to Île de France in March 1796, after a campaign that lasted six months, bringing with him six prizes including the *Triton*, a jewel of the English East India Company. However, the colonial government under Governor Malartic refused to authorise these prizes as Surcouf was not in possession of a letter of marque[31] as required by law. The prizes were therefore confiscated on behalf of the State, and Surcouf drew no profit whatsoever. Furious, he returned to France and got

30. A clearance certificate grants the right to leave port, and is obligatory for all private vessels. It is issued annually for a fixed term in exchange for a fixed sum which is determined by the ship's tonnage.

31. A letter of marque (or of reprisal) promoted the bearer to the rank of privateer, thereby officially authorising him to attack and capture enemy vessels on behalf of the State.

ABOVE: Robert Surcouf's signature.

OPPOSITE (TOP): Port Louis.
*Engraving by Alfred Erny, taken from* Le Tour du Monde, *Librairie L. Hachette et Cie, Paris, 1863.*

OPPOSITE (BOTTOM): The harbour of Port Louis.
*19th-century engraving.*

the authorities to issue a verdict in his favour, which granted him half the value of the prizes. Encouraged by this reversal of fortune, Robert Surcouf returned to Île de France aboard the *Clarisse* in December 1798 but set off again shortly.

He returned to Port Louis in February 1800 with several prizes, enabling him to purchase the *Confiance*. This 490-tonner had 17 cannons and a crew of 204 men composed of 159 Frenchmen, 25 volunteers and 20 settlers from Île de France. It was during a seven-month campaign with the *Confiance*, from April to November 1800, that Captain Surcouf succeeded in boarding and capturing another jewel of the East India Company, the *Kent*, in the Bay of Bengal on 7 October 1800. This 1,200-tonner, equipped with 38 cannons and a crew of 437 soldiers, was undoubtedly the finest prize ever taken by a privateer in the Indian Ocean. After this extraordinary performance, Surcouf returned to St Malo and married the daughter of a rich shipowner, Marie Blaize de Maisonneuve.

**ABOVE:** This pistol, which belonged to Robert Surcouf, is kept in the National History Museum in Mahébourg.

**OPPOSITE:** In 1799, one of Surcouf's colleagues, the privateer Malroux, in charge of the *Amphytrite* fitted with 16 cannons, decided to board the English sloop-of-war the *Trinquemaley*. In desperation, the English captain blew up his ship, which sank straight to the bottom of the sea, taking Captain Malroux with it.

*Drawing by L. Garneray, engraved by Rouargue. France Maritime, 19th century.*

In 1803, England decided that France was not respecting the Treaty of Amiens and, without warning, placed an embargo on all French boats in British ports. Once again, French ships were under systematic attack at sea. At this point Napoleon offered Surcouf the rank of ship's captain in the French Navy. Surcouf brazenly imposed his own conditions, namely to retain his freedom of movement and not be obliged to submit to the orders of the Naval Ministry. The First Consul consequently withdrew its offer.

For three years, Robert Surcouf joined his father-in-law as a shipowner, fitting out several corsairs: the *Caroline*, commanded by his brother Nicolas Surcouf; the *Marsouin*; the *Confiance*, commanded by his cousin Jean-Marie Potier de La Houssaye; and the *Napoléon*, commanded by Malo Le Nouvel. But Robert Surcouf was impatient to get back to sea and decided to build

a vessel that would be the fastest, the easiest to manoeuvre and the best-suited for privateering on the high seas. This 300-tonner named the *Revenant* was soon afloat with 20 cannons and a crew of 192. En route for Île de France he took several prizes, arriving in Port Louis in June 1807 where he met the new governor, General Decaen. In September 1807, he left for the Bay of Bengal for a campaign that lasted four months. By January 1808, Surcouf was back in Île de France, yet again bringing numerous English prizes containing riches and supplies for the island's settlers, who gave him a triumphal welcome.

The privateer was by now 35 years old. He decided to return to France for good, and entrusted the *Revenant* to his cousin, Jean-Marie Potier de La Houssaye. When he learned that an important Portuguese ship, the *Conceçao*, en route from the Cape of Good Hope to India or China was due to be in the vicinity, Surcouf gave Potier instructions to pursue it. However Governor Decean forbade the *Revenant* to depart, and dispatched two of

the navy's frigates to capture the *Conceçao*, only issuing a letter of marque to Captain Potier once they had departed. In spite of this, it was the *Revenant* that succeeded in capturing the *Conceçao*, the two frigates sent by Decaen having failed, and the Portuguese vessel was brought to Port Louis by Potier. To get his revenge for this humiliating turn of events, General Decaen requisitioned the *Revenant* and renamed it the *Iéna*. Surcouf persistently sought justice in this matter, but the governor would not budge. Surcouf therefore purchased a new vessel, the *Sémillante*, which he renamed the *Charles*.

Full of resentment, the privateer decided to return to his native Brittany with his recent prizes – 47 since he started his career. Yet again, the governor intervened and insisted that Surcouf take the captain of the *Conceçao* with him, together with two of his officers. This infuriated Surcouf, who replied that it was highly dangerous for him to carry three officers from a ship that he had captured. But General Decaen would not hear reason. On the day of his departure, Surcouf offloaded the Portuguese officers onto the port's pilot boat and set sail for Brittany. In revenge, the governor confiscated all the privateer's goods on Île de France, but, thanks to his connections, Surcouf managed to get them back. In December 1815, during the Restoration, Decaen, renowned for his loyalty to Napoleon, was arrested and put in prison. Robert Surcouf charitably intervened on his behalf and succeeded in getting the former governor released. From then on, the two men remained on excellent terms.

Decorated with the Legion of Honour, the 'king of privateers' made frequent visits to St Malo to manage his shipowning business. He died of an incurable disease on 8 July 1827, aged 54. His body was transported on a small boat across the bay of St Malo to the cemetery of Rocabey. During the funeral ceremony, tribute was paid to him.

ABOVE: Rosewood desk belonging to Captain Rivington aboard the *Kent*. Robert Surcouf admired it and took it for his personal use.

OPPOSITE: Portrait of Robert Surcouf.
*Engraving by A. Maurin, 1835.*

PAGES 110 & 111: General view of the harbour of Port Louis.
*Engraving by Brager and Sargent, 19th century.*

## Other Privateers in the Indian Ocean

Many other privateers took part in this war of subversion that was fought between France and England during the American War of Independence and then the successive French Revolutionary and Imperial wars.

These sailors were particularly renowned for their bravery and patriotism, and perhaps also for their love of power, glory and money. There were over a hundred of them, of which the following is an inexhaustive list: Nicolas Adam, Antoine Allègre, Guillaume-Marie Angenard, Alexandre Bazin, Dominique Bétuel, Antoine Boichon, Jean-Baptiste Boudin, Étienne Bourgoin, Gabriel de Burguès, Auguste Carosin, Mathurin Carosin, Julien Couloynier, Coutence, Jean Deglo, Jean-Baptiste Dejean Saint-Hilaire, Claude Deschiens de Kérulvay, Jean-Marc Desiest, Julien Desjardins, Pierre Desveaux, Christophe Dubignon, Claude Dubois, Daniel-Marie Dufay de la Branchère, Philippe Dufourq, Jean-Marie Dumaine de La Josserie, Étienne Dupuy, Dutrône, Louis Épron, Antoine Fabre, Ferretier, Jean-Baptiste Fonroque, Cadet de Fontenay, Fournier, Louis Garneray, Félix Grenier Pèzenas, Harel, Haudressy, Thomas Henry, Jean-François Hodoul, Jean-Baptiste Labat, Laboulaye, Charles Guillaume de La Butte, Jacques Lambert, Raphaël Laurent, Louis Leblond, François Legars, François Le Guen de La Croix, Emmanuel Le Joliff, Malo Le Nouvel, Jacques Leroux de Kermorseven, Louis Levaillant, Jean-Louis Loiseau, Jean Mallet, Jean-François Malroux du Bac, Charles Mariette, Millien, Jean Morice, Vincent Moulac, Jean Moulin, Jean Nué, Perron, Paul Pinaud, Piriou de Lezongar, Joseph Potier de La Houssaye, Jacques Prenat, Dominique Quenet, Louis Raguin, Antoine Regnaud de Chandeuil, François Ripaud de Montaudevert, Roux, Jean-Baptiste Rouxel, Auguste Sagory, Charles Surcouf, Emmanuel Surcouf, Nicolas Surcouf, Jean-Baptiste Tabardin, Thréouart de Longpré, Vieillard.

ABOVE (TOP): This street nameplate for the Rue Surcouf in Pondicherry gives some idea of the extent of the privateer's reputation.

ABOVE (BOTTOM): Louis Garneray (1783–1857) operated as a privateer alongside Surcouf and Dutertre until 1806. Imprisoned by the English for eight years, he took up painting and became a marine painter and then a writer. He made the painting of the taking of the *Kent* exhibited in St Malo's history museum.

*Drawing by Biard.*

OPPOSITE: After the heroic boarding and capture of the *Kent*, the pride of the East India Company, Captain Rivington's sabre is handed over to the privateer Robert Surcouf as a sign of capitulation.

*Drawing by Crépin, engraved by Hulk, Paris, 1812.*

## SHIPWRECKS AROUND MAURITIUS

Tales abound of shipwrecks off the shores of the island of Mauritius. The main explanation for these misfortunes can be found in the regular arrival of cyclones every year between December and April. A ship that finds itself running into difficulty in these waters could try to find shelter in one of the two natural harbours that the Mauritian coastline offers, but it would still have reefs to contend with. Naval battles and navigational errors have also led to shipwrecks. One way or another, about a hundred wrecks from various periods have settled on the seabed around Mauritius.

Today, known wrecks of older ships are few and far between, the main ones being the remains of four ships which went down in the 17th and 18th centuries, and three which sank at the beginning of the 19th century, including two in the naval battle of Grand Port.

### The *Banda*

The *Banda* was a vessel belonging to the Vereenigde Oost-Indische Compagnie (VOC), the Dutch East India Company founded in 1602. In 1610, in Bantam (present-day Banten in Indonesia), Admiral Pieter Both was appointed the first Governor-General of the Dutch East Indies, then governed by the VOC. As Governor-General, he managed regional governors, director generals and other agents of the VOC.

Astrolabe with the year 1568 engraved on it, found by Jacques Dumas' team in 1979 on the wreck of the *Banda*. According to Marcel Destombes, expert in the history of maps and scientific instruments, this pre-sextant navigation instrument is probably of Portuguese origin.

At the end of his mandate on 25 December 1614, Both left Bantam for the Netherlands at the head of a small fleet of four ships: the *Banda*, the *Geunieerde Provincien*, the *Gelderland* and the *Delft*. They were either stopping over or sheltering at Noordwester Haven (now Port Louis) when the flotilla was hit by a powerful cyclone. On 6 March 1615, the admiral's ship, the *Banda*, went down off Medine on the west coast of Mauritius with all hands, including Pieter Both, on board. The *Geunieerde Provincien* and the *Gelderland* suffered the same fate. Only the *Delft* made it back to Amsterdam.

It was not until 1979 that divers first demonstrated interest in finding the wreck of the *Banda*. Believing that they could locate the site of the wreck, the Frenchmen Jacques Dumas and Patrick Lizé put together a team which included Mauritians as well as other French divers: Daniel Pélicier, Yves Halbwachs, Sidney Julie and Soriya Gerbié. With the support of UNESCO,

PAGE 116: Aerial photo showing, along the breakers, the Passe Saint-Géran nearly opposite the tip of Île d'Ambre and, further to the left, the Passe des Citronniers where the *Saint-Géran* went down during the night of 17 and 18 August 1744. In the distance, on the Mauritian coast, is the village of Poudre d'Or.

BELOW: The compass was a Chinese invention, introduced to Europe via the Arab world in the 12th century.

OPPOSITE:
1. Pieces of Chinese porcelain from the Ming period (1368–1644) from the wreck of the *Banda*. These are being kept at the Mauritius National History Museum in Mahébourg and at the Blue Penny Museum in Port Louis.

2, 3 & 4. Fragments of Chinese porcelain from the Ming period (1368–1644) from the wreck of the *Geunieerde Provincien*.

PAGE 120: The *Banda* and the *Geunieerde Provincien* were similar to this 17th-century Dutch vessel. *Engraving, late 17th century.*

PAGE 121:
1. & 2. A gold ducat struck during the reign of Francesco Morosini (1688–1694), 108th Doge of Venice, from the wreck of the *Speaker*.

3. A silver French *écu* (circa 1694).

4 & 5. Gold coin from the Ottoman Empire struck in Cairo, found on the wreck of the *Speaker*.

6. A *real*, a Spanish coin, struck in Mexico, from the wreck of the *Speaker*.

7. A thaler, an Austrian coin struck around 1695, during the reign of Leopold I, from the wreck of the *Speaker*.

### The treasure of the *Banda*

The *Banda*, sailing for the VOC, went down on 6 March 1615 off the west coast of Mauritius with Pieter Both, the first Governor-General of the Dutch East Indies, on board. In 1979, the diver Pierre de Sornay found the wreck, and Jacques Dumas and Patrick Lizé's diving team recovered from it pieces of Chinese porcelain from the Ming Dynasty, which today can be seen at the Mauritius National History Museum at Mahébourg and at the Blue Penny Museum at Port Louis.

Armed with a powerful water dredge, metal detectors and a year's worth of perseverance, the team also managed to salvage several valuable artefacts from the wreckage, including 90 pieces of blue-and-white Ming Dynasty porcelain, a Portuguese astrolabe dated 1568, pewter handles from lidded tankards, two pewter spoons with the manufacturer's hallmark still visible, an iron weight, a cannon (probably Swedish), a grappling iron, an anchor weighing one and a half tons, some coins, some nutmegs in a good state of preservation, a small gold chain, some musket balls, a part of a small pewter tap, a set of dividers, a number of pieces of brass in various shapes and sizes and some lead weights.

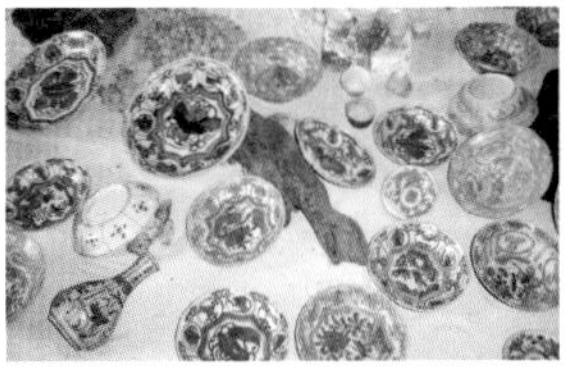
1

2

3

4

they obtained the necessary permits and permission from the Mauritian authorities and, for several weeks, searched for the wreck of the *Banda*, but to no avail. Eventually, it was a Mauritian diver named Pierre de Sornay who showed the team the location of the wreck.

For over three and a half centuries, the *Banda* had lain undisturbed, nearly 30 fathoms deep on the sea floor off Medine on the west coast of Mauritius. The wreck was weighed down by huge rocks that had to be cleared away carefully. Over the centuries, the remains of the ship and its cargo including precious blue-and-white Ming Dynasty porcelain have been strewn about by numerous cyclones.[32]

## The *Geunieerde Provincien*

The *Geunieerde Provincien*, which means 'united provinces' in Dutch, was another ship owned by the VOC, and one of the ships in Pieter Both's

32. Yann von Arnim and Kate Li Kwong Wing, *Blue and White China from Shipwrecks*, Mauritius Museum Council, Mauritius, 2003.

squadron. It now slumbers a few cables' length from the *Banda* on the reef off the beach at Albion. Like the *Banda*, the *Geunieerde Provincien* was transporting a cargo of Chinese blue-and-white porcelain, along with pepper and nutmeg.

According to Pierre de Sornay, "the shipwreck happened over three centuries ago, and, over the years, the ship has totally disintegrated. As a result, it is not really possible nowadays to say that a wreck of the *Geunieerde Provincien* exists as such." Nevertheless, Érick Surcouf, the great-great-great nephew of Robert Surcouf came to Mauritius in 1990 in order to make sure for himself. With his team, he frequently dived on the remains of the *Geunieerde Provincien*. Going over the wreck, Surcouf has been able to identify several elements of the early 17th-century Dutch vessel, as well as to find some nearly intact Ming Dynasty porcelain plates, some lead pigs, and various metal pieces from the vessel and its rigging.

## The *Speaker*

This vessel was a French man-of-war captured on 16 April 1701 by the pirate John Bowen, who took command of her and renamed her the *Speaker*, or the *Speaking Trumpet*.

In April 1702, after some fruitful marauding around the Indian Ocean, Bowen on board the *Speaker* found himself in the vicinity of Île de France at the tail end of the cyclone season. Despite the pirate captain's great experience and seamanship, he could do little against the wild seas. He tried to reach the island and find shelter but, on his approach to the southeast coast, he lost control of his vessel. The *Speaker* ran aground off the mouth of Grande Rivière Sud Est, close to the Îlot des Roches. However, Bowen's efforts to keep the ship afloat ultimately paid off, buying enough time for the crew to build rafts and make it to terra firma, escaping certain death.

1

2

3

4

5

6

7

1

2

3

4

The wreck of the *Speaker* was discovered and explored in 1979 by a team led by Jacques Dumas and Patrick Lizé. Then, in 1990, Érick Surcouf and his team of divers had a go at exploring the wreck. They found several objects that had belonged to Bowen and his crew of 170 pirates: six gold pieces (Venetian ducats and some Islamic dinars), two silver buttons, a gold ingot, a sundial, some musket balls, five sets of dividers, some hand grenades, tobacco pipes, the hilt of a sword, some fragments of pottery and porcelain, some metal deck fittings, some small needles, a lock, two bronze statuettes, and 14 silver coins from India, Spain, the Ottoman Empire, Holland and Austria.

### The *Saint-Géran*

This vessel was a ship owned by the French East India Company.

According to Le Juge de Segrais, "the *Saint-Géran* was launched on 11 July 1736 and fitted out over the following year: a 600-tonner armed with 28 cannons. On her first voyage to Pondicherry, she was commanded by Captain Laurent Aubin Duplessis, leaving Lorient on 11 November 1737 and returning on 14 June 1739. Captain Porée de La Toche then took over as commander. During her third voyage, under the command of Captain Jean Drake, the *Saint-Géran* had to put into port at Île de France due to an epidemic on board."

The vessel was wrecked on the north-northeast coast of Île de France in 1744. At the time, the crew consisted of 149 men under the command of Captain Richard de Lamarre, along with 13 passengers and 30 blacks who had embarked at Gorée [Île de Gorée in Sénégal]. On 17 August 1744 at dusk, the vessel was in sight of the coast and in heavy seas when, being dangerously close to the reefs, she tried to wear ship. As the crew was bringing the mainsail about while tacking to sideboard, the *Saint-Géran* touched bottom and, hit

PAGE 120: The *Banda* and the *Geunieerde Provincien* were similar to this 17th-century Dutch vessel. *Engraving, late 17th century.*

### Those who escaped the shipwreck of the *Saint-Géran*:

Alain Ambroise (boatswain's mate from Port Louis); Pierre Tasset (boatswain's mate from Lorient); Aimé Carret (able seaman from Lorient); Jean Page (sailor from Cleden) ; Jacques Le Guen (sailor and carpenter from Hennebont); Pierre Vergore (gunner from Lorient); Jean Janvrin Daniel, or de Miel (passenger under contract from Saint-Servan); Thomas Chardon (passenger under contract from Hennebont); Diomat (passenger joiner/carpenter from Saumur).

amidships by a huge wave, was thrown onto the reef. The main mast and the mizzenmast were broken. In the panic that followed, the skiffs, rowing boats and dinghies were all destroyed. Thirty-odd people threw themselves into the water and drowned."[33]

The *Saint-Géran* was devastated. That only nine people survived is borne out by a letter from the governor of Île de France, Bertrand François Mahé de La Bourdonnais, to Joseph François Dupleix, Governor-General of French establishments in India, which is partially reproduced below.[34]

*11th September 1744*

*Dear Sir,*

*I have been occupied with salvaging the debris of the Saint-Géran which went down with all hands on board the 15th August last [sic], on our island, save for nine members of its crew of two hundred and sixty [people]. It was not possible to salvage anything from its cargo apart from some odd bits of metal and a few small objects that barely covered the costs of finding them. [...]*

*Mahé de La Bourdonnais*

ABOVE (TOP): Ship's bell from the *Saint-Géran*, currently in the Mauritius National History Museum in Mahébourg.

ABOVE (BOTTOM): Spoon found on the wreck of the *Saint-Géran*.

OPPOSITE:
1. Gold thimble, found on the wreck of the *Saint-Géran*.

2 and 3. Silver Spanish piastre, an 8-*real* coin, the so-called 'piece of eight'. Struck in Mexico in the name of Philip V (1683–1746), King of Spain, and found on the wreck of the *Saint-Géran*.

4. Musket balls from the wreck of the *Saint-Géran*.

33. Le Juge de Segrais, cited in the review *Les Cahiers de l'Iroise*, Société d'Études de Brest et du Léon, 20th century.

34. Raymond Hein, *Le Naufrage du Saint-Géran*, Nathan, Paris, 1981.

The arrival of the *Saint-Géran* had been eagerly anticipated on the island. Mahé de La Bourdonnais himself had ordered some vats and grinding rollers for his sugar estate at La Villebague, which were due to arrive with the ship and which he had been awaiting with great impatience.

A decree passed by the council of Île Bourbon two months after the shipwreck seems to indicate that Mahé de La Bourdonnais also had great need of crates on board the *Saint-Géran* containing 54,000 piastres sent by the French East India Company; its employees had not been paid for more than eight months.

The sinking of the *Saint-Géran* was more, therefore, than just a human tragedy. It also had serious economic repercussions, as can be seen in a letter from Mahé de La Bourdonnais to the governor of Île Bourbon, written in September 1744[35]:

> *It is with sincere regret that we find ourselves facing the impossibility of being able to supply you with wine and flour. The total loss of the vessel the* Saint-Géran *has placed us absolutely outside having the capacity to satisfy your needs, however slightly, with respect to these two articles.*
>
> *The unfortunate vessel was wrecked on the windward side of the island of Ambre on the reefs and in the breakers that reign all through that part of our island.*
>
> *Of two hundred and forty crew and passengers aboard, only nine men came out alive and even less, proportionally, of the goods and cargo.*
>
> *Mahé de La Bourdonnais*

35. This letter comes from the archives of the Léon Dierx Museum in Saint-Denis of Réunion. It was transcribed by G. Suneechur, Director of the National Archives of Mauritius.

For a long time, exploration of the *Saint-Géran*'s wreck produced nothing. In 1964, a team of Mauritian divers led by Paul Fleuriau-Chateau discovered an anchor, a barrel hoop and some ribs from a hull, and brought up some rivets, nails and a rib from a site assumed to be the wreck of the *Saint-Géran*. However, none of the objects were definitively proven to have come from the ship. In 1966, near Île d'Ambre, some divers discovered some pieces of a bronze bell by chance, which proved to belong to the *Saint-Géran*. The bell is now on display at the Mauritius National History Museum in Mahébourg. A few years later, in February 1979, a team of underwater archaeologists led by Jean-Yves Blot recovered a number of objects from the *Saint-Géran* in the Passe des Citronniers near Île d'Ambre, including a gold thimble, a gold buckle, several pulleys, a length of rope, a gun flint, some cannonballs, bits of rigging, a pistol, a hand grenade, some grindstones, some brass nails, some lengths of cloth, a brass needle, a silver handle, a grappling iron, a long pewter spoon, some lead balls, some silver

BELOW: The English frigate HMS *Proserpine* after her capture by the French ship *Pénélope* on 28 February 1809. HMS *Sirius*, also an English frigate, was probably very similar to this ship.

OPPOSITE (TOP): The wrecking of the *Saint-Géran* and the death of Virginie. During his stay on Île de France, Bernardin de Saint-Pierre was inspired by the wrecking to write a novel, *Paul et Virginie*, which has sold over 25 million copies in 30 different languages.

*Lithograph from an original drawing by Joseph Vernet, engraved by Longueil, Paris, 1789.*

OPPOSITE (BOTTOM): Model of the *Saint-Géran*.

*Model made by Historic Marine, Goodlands, Mauritius.*

Spanish piastres, a small silver fork, two copper buttons, a piece of a plate, a silver fork emblazoned with the coat of arms of a certain Monsieur de Bréhan, some French Louis XV coins, a glass carafe stopper, a turned-bronze candelabra and a cross from a rosary.

1

2

3

## HMS *Sirius*

HMS *Sirius* was a 36-gun Royal Navy vessel built in 1797. She was involved in the naval battle of Grand Port from 23 to 26 August 1810.

A few months before English forces took Île de France on 2 December 1810, two naval squadrons, one French and one English, each consisting of four ships, engaged in a fierce battle in the Bay of Grand Port to the southeast of the island. HMS *Sirius* was part of the English squadron under the command of Commodore Samuel Pym. The battle raged for several days before turning to French advantage. On the last day of fighting, the situation was desperate for the English and, rather than let his ship fall into the hands of the French, Captain Pym decided to evacuate it and set it on fire. The fire took hold quickly and the HMS *Sirius* was soon ablaze, finally exploding before foundering on a shoal.

The Mauritius Underwater Group discovered the wreck in 1964, but archaeological work did not get underway until the following year and lasted

### The treasure of HMS *Sirius*

More than 9,000 objects from the wreck of the HMS *Sirius* have been brought to the surface, including an 18-pounder cannon, brass fittings from pistols and English muskets, the gilded part of a dagger scabbard, a French infantry grenadier's sword-hilt, cannonballs, musket balls, parts of the ebony frame of a Hadley's octant, an anchor with a span of over three yards, 30 pulleys, Roman numeral copper draught marks, an Indian 'Pagoda' coin struck in Madras, belt buckles from English uniforms, chest handles, pipes and a door knob with a likeness of Admiral Lord Horatio Nelson embossed upon it.

several years. Despite an unfortunate dynamiting incident in 1968, a major part of the wreck remains in a good state of conservation thanks to the thick coat of silt covering it. Nearly all the objects recovered from the HMS *Sirius* have been incorporated into the collection of the Mauritius National History Museum in Mahébourg.

## HMS *Magicienne*

HMS *Magicienne* was a French 32-gun frigate built at the Toulon naval dockyard in 1778. It was captured on 2 July 1781 by the English Royal Navy ship HMS *Chatham*. Under the command of Captain Lucius Curtis, HMS *Magicienne* was part of the English squadron at the Battle of Grand Port. After two days of intense combat and incessant French cannon fire, the *Magicienne* was in a sorry state. Seeing that the outcome of the battle was already beyond doubt, Curtis decided to abandon his ship and transfer his men to another boat. In order to prevent the *Magicienne* being retaken by the

ABOVE: HMS *Magicienne*, originally a French frigate, was part of the English squadron at the battle of Grand Port.

*Lithograph engraved and drawn by H. Vernon, 19th century.*

OPPOSITE (TOP): A copper coin of the VOC found, curiously enough, on the wreck of HMS *Sirius*.

OPPOSITE (BOTTOM): Nails from the wrecks of HMS *Sirius* (1 and 2) and the *Saint-Géran* (3).

French, Curtis loaded the cannons, had them directed towards the ships of the French squadron, and then set fire to his ship. The fire spread rapidly and immense flames engulfed the frigate, its pre-loaded cannons thundering and roaring away until the inferno reached her magazines, at which point the ship went up in an almighty explosion. During the night of 24 August 1810, the hulk of HMS *Magicienne* foundered in the Bay of Grand Port, leaving only a few bits of debris floating on the surface.

In 1934, the harbour master of Port Louis, H.C.M. Austen, undertook salvage operations on the wreck of the HMS *Magicienne*. From about six fathoms down, and reasonably close to shore, several objects were brought to the surface, including some very well-preserved glass bottles, some English coins, various personal effects of the crew, the rudder post, several cannons and part of thc ship's hull.

## The *Coureur*

The *Coureur* was a two-masted 50-tonner lugger built at Grand Port in 1818. In 1820, Captain Auguste L'Hoste purchased her from her owner, Athanase Touche, and set sail for Africa under the command of Captain Charles Letord, also known as Dorval. On her return from Zanzibar in March 1821, the *Henrietta*, a schooner in the service of the British authorities on Mauritius, gave the *Coureur* chase, as she had been trading in slaves, an illegal activity. On 3 March 1821, the seas were still rough from the recent passage of a cyclone. While trying to escape, Captain Letord misjudged a reef, made a false manoeuvre and hit it, wrecking the *Coureur* off Pointe aux Feuilles, on the east coast of Mauritius. The slaves, numbering about 100, were rescued by the crew, who then set fire to the lugger to destroy any evidence of slave-trading, hoping to avoid legal proceedings with the English authorities in Mauritius.

ABOVE: A wine bottle from the late 18th to early 19th century, found on one of the wrecks off the coast of Mauritius.

OPPOSITE: The wreck of the *Coureur*, discovered in October 2004 by Armiyo Vurdapa Naiken on the east coast of Mauritius, opposite Pointe aux Feuilles.

In October 2004, a diver discovered a wreck at Pointe aux Feuilles that was subsequently confirmed, the *Coureur*, by a team that included Yann von Arnim, an underwater archaeologist and Vice-President of the Mauritius Marine Conservation Society. Over 7,000 objects have been recovered from the wreakage, including fragments of crude blue-and-white Chinese porcelain, musket balls, part of a pendant, copper nails, chain links probably used to restrain the slaves, pulleys, gun flints and a pewter plate.

## Other Wrecks

There are many other wrecks around the island of Mauritius. The *Sumatra* went down near Île Plate (Flat Island) in 1750; the *Neptune* was wrecked in the same year; and the *Ambulante* sank near Le Morne Brabant in 1774.

Bernardin Nageon de l'Étang, so the story goes, wrecked his ship at Pointe Vacaos, not far from the shore, towards the middle of the 18th century. The

## Wrecks in Port Louis

During the 18th century, when Île de France belonged to the French, it became the default port of call for ships criss-crossing the Indian Ocean. In 1775, Monsieur de Boisquenay, captain of a fireship, carried out a survey of the carcasses of ships that had sunk in the harbour at Port Louis and that had, over time, become consolidated enough to serve as potential anchor or mooring points for other ships. Thanks to de Boisquenay, therefore, we have an accurate chart from this period of exactly where each wreck lies in the harbour silt.

Here is the list: the *Fière*, the *Renommée*, the *Colombe*, the *Clotilde*, the *Bourbon*, the *Danaé*, the *Saint Philippe*, the *Aigle*, the *Maurepas*, the *Walpoole*, the *Centaure*, the *Vigilant*, the *Illustre*, the *Grantham*, the *Désir*, the *Machault*, the *Bertin*, the *Auguste*, the *Fulvie*, the *Choiseul*, the *Nécessaire*, the *Pénélope*, the *Mars*, the *Corisante*, the *Moras*, the *Seychelles*, the *Duc d'Anjou*, the *Duc d'Orléans*, the *Duc de Bourgogne*, and two Dutch flutes, the *Reine* and the *Silhouette*.

ship was carrying gold, pearls, emeralds and diamonds from the mines of Golconda and Visapoor in India and, according to some, this treasure was hidden in a safe place in a cave somewhere in the interior of the island.

A bit further out, in the archipelago of Saint Brandon, sometimes known as Cargados Carajos, to the northeast of Mauritius, there are several other wrecks including a 16th-century Portuguese vessel, the *Bom Jesus*, which sank in 1591; and a 17th-century Dutch ship, the *Arnheim*, which went down in 1662. Île de Sable (present-day Tromelin Island), one of the Îles Éparses, is the site of the wreck of the *Utile*, a French slaver. She loaded up with slaves in Madagascar and ran aground on the reefs of Île de Sable on her way to Île de France. Taking refuge on the island, the crew built a boat on which they travelled back to Madagascar, leaving the 60 slaves behind but promising to return.

They never did. Fourteen years later, in 1775, Captain Bernard-Marie Boudin de Tromelin (after whom the island was renamed) visited the island and rescued the survivors: one man, seven women and an eight-month-old baby. The position of the wreck has been pinpointed by a team of French meteorologists working on Tromelin Island.

ABOVE: The octant, ancestor of the sextant and a vital navigation instrument for seafarers, was invented in 1730 by the Englishman John Hadley.
*Spencer, Browning & Co, London, c 1840.*

OPPOSITE: In his novel *Paul et Virginie*, Bernardin de Saint-Pierre took some liberties with Mauritius' geography. Virginie is shipwrecked on the east coast, yet her body is found "in the bay next to the valley of the River des Lataniers", on the west coast of the island.

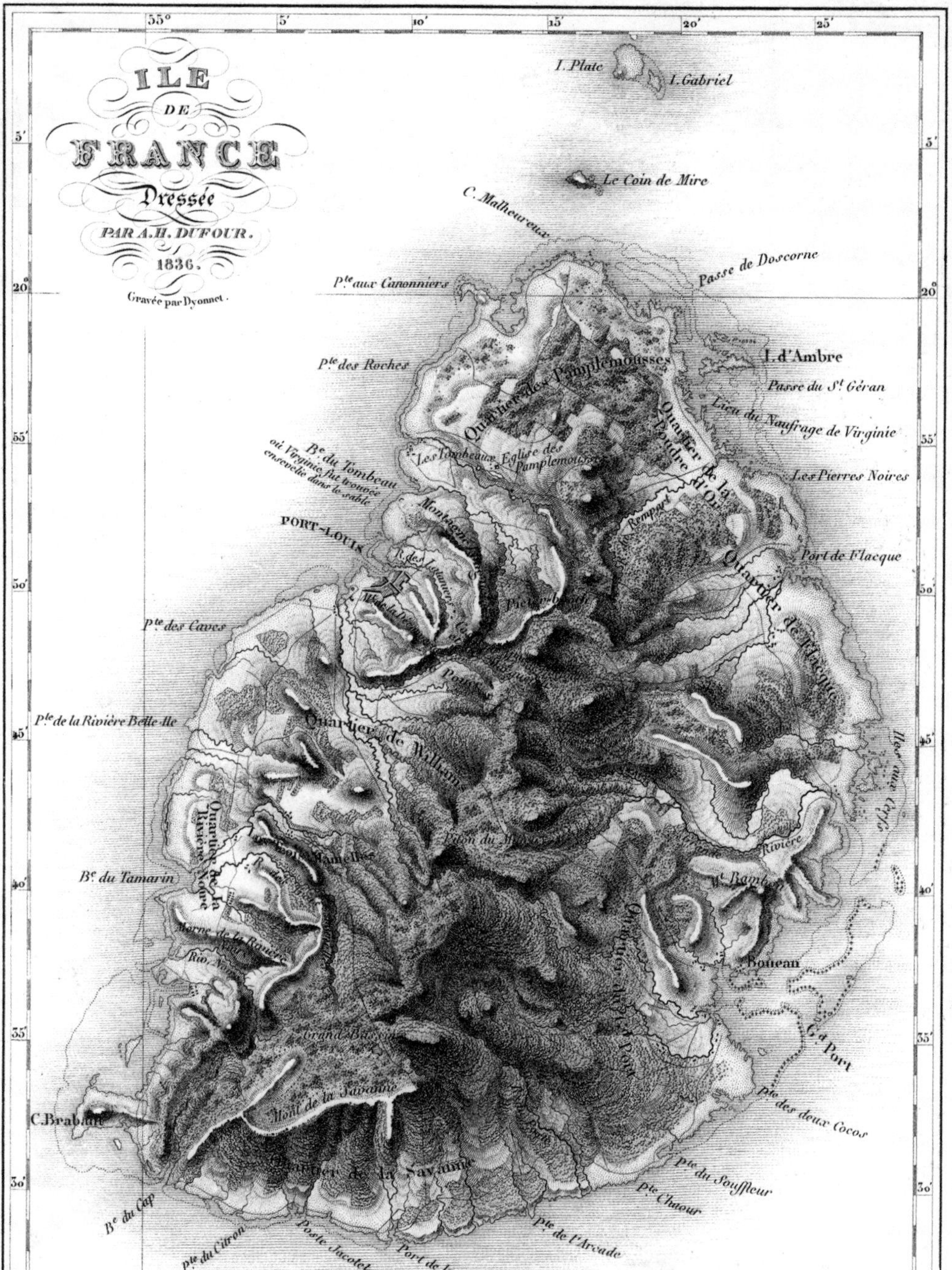


Ecrit par Hacq.

# ARRIVALS, DEPARTURES AND SALE OF PRIVATEER VESSELS IN PORT LOUIS (1797–1810)

The following information is for the most part derived from the *Gazette de l'île de France*, compiled by an anonymous author, and has been reproduced here in a reorganised manner for greater clarity. The style and vocabulary of the period have, however, been respected where possible.

**THE YEAR OF 1797**

* The *Cornwallis*, prize of the *Entreprise*, arrived 25 January, Captain Leblond [two other prizes had been sent to Île de France by Legars, captain of the *Entreprise*].
* The *Kaunitz*, under a Genovese flag, prize of the *Entreprise*, arrived 26 January, commanded by Haudressy, with wine, beer, iron and sails on board.
* The *Entreprise*, Captain Legars, arrived 9 February.
* An English vessel captured by Perroud on the coast of Orissa, arrived 14 February, commanded by Pascal, with merchandise from India and some opium.
* The *Éliza*, English prize of 450 tons taken in the Malacca Straits by the *Modeste*, Captain Dutertre, arrived 15 February, commanded by Lemener, with merchandise from India, opium, lacquer and arrack [Dutertre took two other prizes, one of which was expedited to Aceh and the other to Île de France].
* The *Castor*, a 150-tonner English brig, captured by the schooner *Hay*, Captain Perroud, arrived 17 February, Captain Hodoul, with a cargo of wheat and rice.
* The *Émilie Gest*, an English snow-brig, prize of the *Modeste*, sent from Achem [Aceh] 29 December, arrived 24 February, commanded by Abadie, with wheat, rice, fabrics and Madeira wine on board.
* The schooner *Hay*, prize of the *Entreprise*, arrived 5 March, Captain Perroud.
* The *Apollon*, departed 7 March with 71 men.
* The brig *Etimbeth*, arrived from Pagu 6 April, Captain Langlard, purchased with the proceeds of the sale of the *Alcyon*, Captain Dufourq.
* The *Nostra Senhora Darabida*, a Portuguese vessel, captured on 24 March off the coast of Mozambique by the *Embuscade*, Captain Duchaussy, arrived 4 May in ballast, commanded by Captain Auger, with 30,000 piastres on board taken by the *Embuscade*.
* The *Ferté*, prize of the *Modeste*, arrived 6 May, Captain Girardot, with a cargo of rice.
* The *Aydresev*, a vessel of approximately 500 tons, under the Marath flag, captured on 17 May near Mazulipatam by the *Apollon*, Captain Hodoul, arrived 23 June. Captain Harel, who commanded this prize, stated that on 3 May the *Apollon* had taken over an English vessel on its way to Tranquebar.
* The *Maraq*, English vessel captured by the *Apollon*, arrived 14 July, commanded by Étienne Dupeyré.
* The *Thomas*, English prize of the *Brûle-Gueule*, arrived 9 October with 620 bales of merchandise composed of sugar, indigo and saltpetre.
* The *Harrington*, an English schooner, captured by the *Apollon* on 9 November off Sand Heads of the Bay of Bengal, arrived 21 December, Captain Nicolas Montalent.
* The sloop the *Risque*, prize taken by the *Forte* and the *Prudente* near Madras on 21 November, arrived 23 December.
* The *Greenwich*, captured on 25 November at the southern tip of Ceylon by the *Forte* and the *Prudente* [which that same day also took the

PAGES 133 & 134: Drawing by H. Simoni on the occasion of the bicentenary of the birth of Charles Beautemps-Beaupré (1766–1854), French hydrographic engineer and cartographer.
*Naval Hydrographic Service.*

OPPOSITE: Port Louis, Île de France.
*Drawing by Alfred Paris, engraved by Himely, taken from* Voyage autour du Monde de la Corvette La Favorite, *Captain Laplace, Éditions de Sainson, 1830–1832.*

View of a street in Port Louis.
*Drawing by Alfred Erny, taken from* Le Tour du Monde, *Librairie L. Hachette et Cie, Paris, 1863.*

*Pigot*, sailing from Bombay to Calcutta with merchandise and 94,000 rupies, and which was expedited to Batavia in order to drop off some passengers and the Cochin garrison which was on board], commanded by Captain Fichet.

**THE YEAR OF 1798**

* A vessel under an Arab flag, apprehended and expedited on 28 November by the *Forte*, being without papers, arrived 1 January with a cargo of wheat.
* The *Apollon*, Captain Hodoul, arrived 7 January with 57 prisoners and 50,000–60,000 piastres coming from the *Rey*, captured in the shallows [of the Bay of Bengal] and abandoned 20° North.
* The *Loret*, a 400-tonner, captured by the *Apollon* off Sand Heads of the Bay of Bengal, arrived 18 January.
* The *Petit Volcan*, an 80-tonner English brig captured by Captain Ripaud de Montaudevert, arrived 19 January, commanded by the latter, with two of Tippoo Sultan's ambassadors.
* The *Jeune Adèle*, Captain Ripaud Lecotais, departed from Réunion on 25 June and the Seychelles on 19 July, where it only made a port of call, as it was re-bound for Réunion, arrived 17 August.
* The *Samad Jenny*, an 800-tonner, flying the flag of the Queen of Cannanore [now Kannur], apprehended on 4 August in the Red Sea by the *Uni*, arrived 12 September, Captain Desjardins.
* The *Uni*, Captain Le Même, arrived 12 November, for a port of call.
* The *Clarisse*, Captain Robert Surcouf, departed from Nantes on 18 August, arrived 5 December. Captured two English vessels and two Portuguese vessels, three of which were scuppered.
* The *Louisia*, a Danish vessel, departed from Ceylon on 24 October, arrived 4 December, Captain Baudin. Having been apprehended near the Seychelles by the English vessel *Centurion*, which took it to Ceylon, whence it was expedited bound for the Cape of Good Hope. [On 22 November, Baudin and his ten-men crew took possession of it by night. The *Centurion* had gone to the Seychelles to capture a Danish vessel which was known to be carrying a lot of money. On board the *Louisia* there were 20 men from the Centurion. The money was sent from Ceylon to Madras by the English, while awaiting a decision regarding its confiscation.]

**THE YEAR OF 1799**

* The *Éliza*, an English prize, departed from Saint-Denis on 18 January, arrived on 26 January.
* The *Concorde*, from China, prize taken by the *Prudente* on Agulhas Bank, arrived on 10 March.
* The *Catherine*, English prize, expedited 9 February, arrived on 1 April, Captain Fautrel, with merchandise from China.
* A vessel commanded by Captain Collet, arrived 4 April.
* The *Surprise*, a 500-tonner prize, taken in the shallows of the Bay of Bengal on 4 March by the *Forte*, which took two other prizes, arrived 6 April, Captain Lespiau, with a cargo of rice.
* The *Anna Maria*, captured on 18 February, arrived 8 April, Captain Desjardins, with a cargo of pepper.
* The *Humber*, English prize commanded by Captain Dutertre, arrived 20 April with a cargo of linen, silk, wine, etc.
* The *Yarmouth*, captured in the shallows of the Bay of Bengal by the *Forte* on 20 February, arrived 23 April.
* The *Mornington*, a 600-tonner, captured in the shallows of the Bay of Bengal by the *Forte* on 5 March, arrived 23 April.
* The *Marguerite*, an English three-master, expedited on 25 April, arrived 4 June, Captain Mathurin Carosin.
* The *Diana*, an 80-tonner, expedited on 25 April, arrived 9 June, Captain Grenier.
* The *Clarisse*, Captain Robert Surcouf, departed from Réunion on 8 June, where it had taken shelter for a month, chased by a passing vessel near Île de France, arrived 10 June.
* The *Amirbux*, under a Moor flag, expedited from the coast of Sumatra on 13 April, arrived 30 June, Captain Dumaine.
* The *Flore*, a Portuguese vessel, expedited on 17 May, arrived 4 August, commanded by Sauldrier, with fabrics and rum.
* The *Hasard*, from Batavia, expedited on 15 July, arrived 3 September.
* A Portuguese prize, arrived 30 September, Captain Mignot.

* The *Uni*, Captain Le Même, arrived 25 October.
* The *Rudenmark*, a Danish vessel, arrived 31 October with a cargo of fabrics.
* The *Notre-Dame du Bon Succès*, a Portuguese vessel, departed from Lisbon on 21 May, arrived 4 November with 86,000 piastres, 250 bottles of wine, etc.
* An English prize, arrived 22 November, Captain Verchin.
* The *Perle*, prize of the *Iphigénie*, Captain Ripaud de Montaudevert, arrived 26 November.
* The *Nadabeth*, expedited on 6 October, arrived 29 November, Captain Auffray, with a cargo of sugar.

**THE YEAR OF 1800**

* The *Ampillier*, expedited on 11 November 1799, arrived 6 January, Captain Harel, after making a port of call in Réunion, with 600 milliers of rice, 300 crates of sugar and rum.
* The *Caderbaux*, under a Moor flag, arrived 15 January, Captain Adam.
* The sloop *Consolante*, made from remnants of the *Éclair*, arrived 4 February.
* The *Clarisse*, Captain Robert Surcouf, arrived 6 February, with 34,000 piastres derived from his prizes.
* The *Louise de Balnmore*, expedited on 6 January, arrived 11 February with merchandise.
* The *Confiance*, Captain Vaudin, arrived 3 March with 4,000 piastres derived from his prizes.
* The *Mercure*, a Portuguese vessel, arrived from Macao on 6 March, Captain Montalent, with sugar, indigo and Chinese porcelain.
* The *Général Malartic*, Captain Dutertre, arrived 9 March.
* The *Jane*, captured on 1 January in the shallows of the Bay of Bengal, with rice, sugar and bales of merchandise, arrived 9 March, Captain Arnulphy, having made a port of call in Réunion.
* The *Fatasalem*, English prize taken on 25 December 1799 by Captain Dutertre, arrived 22 March with calin [alloy of lead and tin], pepper, sago, arrack, etc.
* *The Élizabeth*, captured in January off the Coromandel Coast, arrived 28 March, Captain Drogard, with rice, wheat, cotton, tar and wine.
* The *Hasard*, departed from Réunion on 29 May, arrived 4 June, unable to reach Tranquebar as a result of its chases.
* The *Diane*, arrived 12 July, for a port of call, with a Portuguese prize.
* The *Arménien*, English prize of the *Clarisse*, Captain Le Même, expedited on 7 July, arrived 17 July, Captain Fabre.
* The *Marquis de Wellesley*, captured near Vingapatnam [Visakhapatnam] on 10 September by the *Général Malartic*, arrived 28 October, Captain Mariette, with 200 milliers of wheat, rice, etc.
* The *Gouverneur Roth*, Captain Adam, arrived 18 November with rice.
* The *Confiance*, Captain Robert Surcouf, arrived 18 November.
* The *Kent*, Captain Drieu, and another vessel commanded by Lefèvre.
* The *Henriette*, Captain Pépin, captured in the shallows of the Bay of Bengal on 24 September, arrived 2 December, with rice.
* The *Voyageur*, Captain Macquet, arrived 12 December with 110,000 piastres.
* The *Harriet*, English ship formerly the *Augustine*, captured in the Seychelles, expedited 1 June, arrived 2 July, commanded by Lebas, naval pupil.

**THE YEAR OF 1801**

* The *Amboina*, captured within sight of the coast of Arakan at 20° North on 14 November, arrived 3 January, Captain Dufay, with paving stones, iron, nails, fabrics, wheat, tobacco and opium.
* The *Persévérant*, captured whilst stranded off Achem [Aceh] on 10 November 1800, arrived 24 January, Captain Cousinery, with salt and fabrics.
* The *Frederick Nord*, captured in the shallows of the Bay of Bengal on 2 January, arrived 11 February, Captain Lamarre, with money-cowry shells.
* The *Malacca*, captured off the Malabar Coast on 22 December, arrived 15 February, Captain Gobin, with pitch.
* The sloop *Athènes*, Captain Frémont, who was obliged to abandon it, arrived 20 February.
* The *Pégou*, captured on 5 February leaving Martaban, arrived 25 March, Captain Aubert, with machines, planks, etc.
* The *May Florence*, captured near Masulipatam, with arrack etc., Captain Maupassant.
* The *Diana*, captured on 26 January in the Pagu shallows, arrived 27 April, Captain Button, with

ABOVE: Whilst French corsairs, based on Île de France, were going about their business in the Indian Ocean, Toussaint Louverture, born in the French colony of Saint-Domingue (present-day Haiti) in 1743, was proclaimed Lieutenant Governor of the island in 1796, and then commander-in-chief of the army. In 1801, he was appointed Captain General of Saint-Domingue by Napoleon himself, but he led the revolution for the independence of the island. In October 1802, this brilliant military leader (and former slave) was arrested by the French Republican forces led by Napoleon Bonaparte's brother-in-law, General Charles Leclerc. He was immediately exiled to France and imprisoned in Fort de Joux (Jura), where he died in 1803.

*Lithograph by Delpech, 19th century, Paris.*

OPPOSITE: *Battle of Grand Port, Île de France, by Louis Lebreton (1818–1866), painter, engraver and lithographer.*

*A.Gosselin Imprimeur et Éditeur, Paris.*

resin, pepper and Chinese porcelain.

* The galley *Diane*, Captain Moulin, returning from privateering, moored at Grand Port 23 May, arrived at Port Louis 31 May. Took three prizes which are all expected.
* The *Nymphe*, Captain Coutance, departed from the Seychelles on 7 May, arrived 9 June.
* The *Good Hope*, Captain Fruchard, having made a port of call in Réunion, arrived 21 June with rice, wood, sailcloth and musket balls.
* The *Bellone*, a 700-tonner, departed from Calcutta on 10 March, captured by the *Chiffone* in the Mozambique canal on 16 June, arrived 15 July with sugar, indigo, pepper, cinnamon and silks.
* The *Orient*, captured on 6 October, arrived 14 November, Captain Leroux, with 6,000 sacks of rice.
* The *Clarisse*, Captain Casting, captured on 16 October, arrived 16 November with sugar, mirrors and 220 musket balls.
* The *Prince*, vessel of the East India Company [probably the English one], Captain Pineau, departed from Madras escorted by the *Suffolk*, a warship with 380 French prisoners on board, arrived 20 November.
* The galley *Nancy*, captured in Bengal on 11 October, arrived 27 November, Captain Julien, with 1,800 sacks of rice, 1,000 sacks of wheat, 24 pipes [barrel containing slightly less than 600 bottles] of Madeira and 70 crates of silk.
* The *Sophie*, captured in the shallows of the Bay of Bengal on 26 October, arrived 14 December, Captain Deville, with three bales of merchandise from India, iron and rum.

**THE YEAR OF 1802**

* The *Petit Cornwallis*, taken by the French prisoners who were on board, arrived 7 February, Captain Gautier.
* The *Amboina*, Captain Aubert, arrived 8 February with 200 bales of fabrics.
* The *England*, Captain Luco, arrived 12 March with objects from Europe.
* The *Bellone*, returned 3 April, one of its prizes, the *Farquhar*, arrived 2 April with saltpetre, rice, cotton, sugar, indigo, Madeira and muslin.
* A prize commanded by Captain Dumaine, arrived 10 April with saltpetre, pepper, indigo, sago, canvas, etc.
* The *Jamy*, arrived 24 April with 250 sacks of benzoin [gum].
* The *Subtil*, returned 29 April.
* The *Actif*, prize of the *Subtil*, arrived 3 May with pepper, sugar and calin.
* The *Penang*, arrived 18 May with sugar, pepper, cloves and earthenware.

**THE YEAR OF 1806**

* The *Piémontaise*, Captain Épron, arrived 4 July, departed from Port Nord-Ouest 7 June, with its prize, the *Warren Hastings, a 1,300–1,400-tonner East Indiaman armed with 18 cannons and merchandise from China*. [The *Warren Hastings* was shipwrecked on Île Bourbon during a cyclone at the end of the month of December 1806, having been sold on 11 December, with its apparel and tackle.]
* Arrival 29 August of the English prize the *James Decamen*, captured by the frigate *Sémillante*, laden with cotton, myrrh, sections of sandalwood trunks and shark's fins.
* Arrival 24 November of the *Actéon*, prize of the frigate *Sémillante*, and of the *Rahim Shaw* (under a Moor flag), prize of the frigate *Piémontaise*; the *Actéon* laden with bales of merchandise, pepper, opium, etc, and the *Rahim Shaw* with copper lining, copper nails, tea, mercury, iron and 22 horses.
* Arrival 1 December of the frigate *Sémillante* and of the *Famma*, an English prize of the frigate *Piémontaise*.
* The *Napoléon*, prize of the *Diamant*, consignees the Lenouvel brothers, three-masted vessel, of about 400 tons, copper-lined, to be sold 5 April by notary Guérin.
* *The Île de France*, Captain J.T. David, shipowner Alexis François Leclézio (9 April 1806).
* *The Henriette*, Captain A. Sagory, consignee Claude Georges Barillon (16 April 1806).
* *The Bellone*, Captain Perroud, consignees Tabois Dubois & Cie (9 April 1806).
* *The Bellone*, sale 30 May 1806 of the effects, linen and duds [old clothes] of Jean Blanchet, Pierre Euget, Jean Salabardeuc, Henri Benyon, Joseph Alouze and John Anson, who were part of the crew of this privateer.

* The *Émilien*, privateer, formerly the *Gloire*, shipowner C.F. Boudret, will depart in a few days (9 July 1806).
* The *Deux Sœurs*, privateer, Captain Dejean-Hilaire, shipowners Loirette and Martineau, will depart next week (23 July 1806).
* The *Lady William Bentings*, prize of the *Bellone*, arrived 17 August with pepper, benzoin and pitch.
* The *Henry Addington*, prize of the privateer *Manchot*, arrived 27 August, laden with merchandise from China.
* The *Manchot*, two-masted privateer, of about 60 tons, copper lined, with its apparel, tackle, weapons and utensils, marked up for sale on 29 August 1806.
* The *Orient*, prize taken by the privateer *Bellone*, consignees Tabois Dubois & Cie, merchants, Place de l'Église; sale on 8 September of the cargo, consisting of rice, wheat and sugar. Delivery, either to the warehouses or to the Rivière-Noire, to be decided by the purchasers.
* The *John Drumont*, sale 24 September 1806 of the merchandise of this prize in the prize warehouse, near the hospital.
* The sloop *Émilien*, an 18-gun privateer with a crew of 150 men, was captured by the English vessel *Culloden* after a chase that lasted two days and one night, 25 September at two in the morning, near the huts on Godavari Point [Cape Godavari]. During the chase, the privateer ran aground during the night. To right itself, it jettisoned 12 of its cannons overboard and lost its anchors and small boats. The *Émilien* had previously been the English sloop *Trinquemaley*. It was copper-lined and reputed to be one of the finest privateers in Île de France. It had already troubled English trade whilst called the *Gloire*. It left the islands two months ago and had not yet taken any prizes (10 December 1806).
* The *Manchot*, Sirs Marius Thomassin, who commands it, and Jacques André Leroy, writer, planned departure 15 October 1806.
* The *Sir Lawrence Pearson*, prize of the privateer *Bellone*. Some merchandise was sold 30 September by the consignees Tabois Dubois & Cie, who will also sell the *Sir Lawrence Pearson* and the *Orient*, both three-masters, at the end of October.
* The *Manchot*, privateer, shipowner Geminard. Notice for suppliers (5 November 1806).
* The *Henry Addington*, English three-master, of about 350 tons, copper-lined, with its apparel, tackle etc, and its cargo, consisting of pepper, wheat, paving stones, iron, steel, etc, to be sold on 6th November, at the behest of Pierre Geminard, owner of the privateer *Manchot* (5 November 1806).
* Sale announced for 30 November, in Saint-Paul, Île Bonaparte [Réunion], at the behest of the owner of the privateer *Manchot*, of the brig *Kable*, an English prize, with its apparel, tackle etc, and 13 chests of opium and 12 chests of saffron from the English prize *Henry Addington* (19 November 1806).
* The *Patrice Salem*, an Arab prize, coming from Pulopinang [Penang], arrived 22 December with some pitch, pepper, rattan, calin [alloy of lead and tin], stained woods, paving stones, etc.
* Sale 26 December at the prize warehouse, of the *Actéon* and of the *Fame*, copper-lined prizes, with their apparel, etc.

**THE YEAR OF 1807**

* The *Mustapha*, a 600–700-tonner, built of teak, copper-lined, prize of the *Deux Sœurs*, Captain Dejean-Hilaire, shipowners Martineau and Loirette, offered for sale 19 February.
* Prize of the *Fatal Barry*, an Arab vessel arrived

22 November 1806 with a cargo of old iron, arsenic, soda, blocks of solid silver worth 4,986 piastres, old jewellery and burned military stripes, offered for sale 6 February.

* Sale 12 March of the privateer *Manchot*, a brig of roughly 60 tons, at the behest of Pierre Geminard, shipowner.
* Sale in Saint-Paul, Île Bonaparte [Réunion], of the cargo of the vessel the *Kaderbacah*, prize of the privateer *Vigilant*, equipped by Hoareau and commanded by Jean Nué (25 March).
* The privateer *Adèle*, shipowner Bonaffé, due to set sail in early July, requests 15 Mozambicans to join its crew (24 June).
* Sale 3 July at the behest of the Lenouvel brothers, consignatories of the privateers *Caroline* and *Napoléon*, of twelve 36-pounder bronze carronades, two 1-pounder bronze cannons for stone cannonballs, and six 6-pounder iron cannons, with gun carriages, cannonballs, bullets and utensils.
* Projected departures: the privateer *Bonne Aventure*, 29 July, Curé and Bouchaud shipowners and Julien Jouan Desjardins captain; 5 August, Joseph Marie Thomassin, former captain of the *Manchot*; 12 August, Vincent Moulac, naval officer; 26 August, Laurent Pinaud, captain; 30 September, François Legars, captain; Louis Moulin, merchant navy captain [no date].
* At the behest of the shipowners of the *Fatal Barry*, sale announced for 12 September, blocks of solid silver worth 4,986 piastres, some old jewellery and burned military stripes, as well as 1,200 lbs of gunpowder from the *Mustapha*.
* Loirette invites those who wish to make claims concerning the *Kaderbacak*, prize of the privateer *Vigilant*, to make themselves known (9 September).
* Henri Hoareau, owner of the *Vigilant*, invites the bearers of shares of the aforesaid privateer to make themselves known at Loirette (11 November).
* Planned departure of Julien Barthélemy Nué, naval captain (23 December).
* The *Revenant*, Captain Robert Surcouf, consignee Guillaume Lenouvel. Prizes: the *Trafalgar*, a three-master of roughly 800 tons, copper-lined, with 10,000 sacks of rice from Bengal; the *Maingless*, a three-master, copper-lined, also with 10,000 sacks of rice from Bengal, books, mirrors and furniture; and the *Suzanne*, a 400-tonner three-master, copper-lined, with rice and sailcloth (11, 18 and 25 November, and 2 and 16 December).
* 12 March: sale, by order of the colonial prefect, of the prize *Nancy* and its cargo of pepper, dry pitch, opium, benzoin and coffee.
* 8 June: sale of the three-master *Cusruphy*, of roughly 400 tons, built of teak, with apparel.
* 14 November: sale of the merchandise from the *Althéa* and the *Élisabeth*, prizes taken by the frigate *Sémillante*, consisting of bales of canvas, opium, lacquer sticks, raw silk, curry powder, paving stones, garlic and ginger (11 November).
* 5 December: sale of the merchandise from the *Giwell*, prize of the *Sémillante* (2 December).
* 10 December: sale of the merchandise from the cargoes of the *Louise*, the *Caroline* and the *Ressource*, prizes taken by the *Sémillante* and the *Piémontaise* (9 December).
* 25 December: sale of 700 sacks of dhal [tropical leguminous plant] in the form of seeds from the prizes *Piémontaise*, and of 1,200 bales and 170 half-bales of cotton wool from the *Althéa* (23 December 1807).
* 31 December: sale of the merchandise from the prizes of the *Piémontaise*, consisting of 11 bales of raw silk, 1,700 bales and half-bales of cotton wool from Bengal, 26 chests of rum and eau-de-vie [fruit brandy], 150 sacks of dhal and 37 sacks of curry powder. The rice from the *Piémontaise* was acquired by the administration (23 December).

**THE YEAR OF 1810**

* The *Henry*, Captain Perrot, shipowner Bonaffé. Prizes: the *Dady Lahy*, with a cargo of blue canvas, percale, etc, and the *Ramshandrak* (13 and 18 July).
* The *Olivor*, a three-master, captured by the sloop *Entreprenant* and renamed the *Jeune Camille*, must leave shortly for France under the orders of Victor Deglos. Shipowners Pitot and Cloupet (25 July).
* The *Swift*, renamed the *Athalante*, Sitzler & Cie shipowners, must leave for France in July.
* The *Confiance*, Captain Thomassin, shipowner Jean Esparon. Prize: the three-master *Philip Dundas*, a 350–400-tonner English vessel, in teak, copper-lined. Cargo: 15 chests of opium, 200 pieces of satin, silk and blue fabric, 150 lbs of cloves, etc. (10 October).

# BIBLIOGRAPHY


ARNIM, Yann von, LI Kwong Wing, Kate, *Blue and White China from Shipwrecks in Mauritius, Indian Ocean*, Mauritius Museum Council, Mauritius, 2003.

AUSTEN, H.C.M., *Sea Fights and Corsairs of the Indian Ocean,* R.W. Brooks, Govt. Printer, Mauritius, 1934.

BELLEC, François, *Les Esprits de Vanikoro, le mystère Lapérouse*, Gallimard, Paris, 2006.

BLOT, Jean-Yves, *À la Recherche du Saint-Géran*, Arthaud, Paris, 1984.

BONAPARTE, Roland Prince, *Premier établissement des Néerlandais à Maurice*, Paris, 1890.

BONO, Salvatore, *Les corsaires en Méditerranée*, Paris-Méditerranée, Paris, 2000.

CARTER, Marina, *Pirates of Mauritius*, Pink Pigeon Press, London, 2003.

CHAZAL, Gaëtan de, *Histoire maritime des Mascareignes*, Éditions du Corsaire, Mauritius, 2007.

COLLECTIF, *Les Anneaux de la mémoire*, CIM, Corderie Royale, Rochefort, 1992.

COLLECTIF, catalogue, *Les Maquettes Comajora*, Precigraph Ltée, Pailles, 1976.

COLLECTIF, *Dictionnaire de biographie mauricienne*, Port-Louis, Mauritius: ADOLPHE, Harold, and D'UNIENVILLE, Raymond (Betia or Bety, M.E. Sobobie: No. 35, 1975, p.1022); BECHET Octave (J.F. Perroud: No. 29, 1967, p. 863); RÉGNARD, L. Noël (F.Y. Carosin: No. 28, 1966, p. 826); TOUSSAINT, Auguste (J. Bowen: No.14, 1944, p. 419; F.T. Le Même: No. 2, 1941, p. 53; J.M. Drieu: No. 40, 1984, p. 1205; J.M. Dutertre: No. 16, 1945, p. 485, R. Surcouf No. 3,1941, p. 93).

COLLECTIF, *Diodon Bulletin*, Mauritius Underwater Group, Phoenix, Mauritius.

COLLECTIF, *Histoire de la marine,* L'illustration, Paris, 1934.

COMBEAUD, Bernard, *Bordeaux corsaire*, Mollat, Bordeaux, 1993.

CUNAT, Charles, *Histoire de Robert Surcouf*, La Découvrance, Rennes, 1994.

DEFOE, Daniel, *A General History of the Pyrates*, J.M. Dent & Sons, London, 1972.

DESCHAMPS, Hubert, *Les pirates à Madagascar*, Berger-Levrault, Paris, 1972.

DESCHAMPS, Hubert, *Pirates et flibustiers*, Presses Universitaires de France, Paris, 1973.

DUMAS, Jacques, *Fortune de mer à l'île Maurice*, Atlas Films, Paris, 1981.

EXEQUEMELIN, Alexandre-Olivier, *Histoire des aventuriers flibustiers d'Amérique*, La Découvrance, La Rochelle, 2006.

FILLIOT, Jean-Michel, *Histoire des Seychelles*, Jouve, Paris, 1983.

FLEURIAU-CHATEAU, Paul, *Aventures en mer*, Éditions Le Printemps, Mauritius, 2001.

GARNERAY, Louis, *Corsaire de la République*, Payot, Paris, 1991.

GARNERAY, Louis, *Le négrier de Zanzibar*, Payot, Paris, 1992.

GARNERAY, Louis, *Pirates et négriers*, Éditions La Nouvelle France, Paris, 1954.

GARNERAY, Louis, *Un corsaire au bagne*, Payot, Paris, 1992.


View of Grand Port, near Mahébourg.

*Drawing by Alfred Erny, taken from* Le Tour du Monde, *Librairie L. Hachette et Cie, Paris, 1863.*

ABOVE: Small nails made of a copper alloy, covered in verdigris, from the wreck of HMS *Sirius*.

OPPOSITE: View over Port Louis from Montagne des Signaux. The church of Saint Louis is clearly visible, as is, in the distance, the causeway built between 1772 and 1781 by Bernard Marie Boudin de Tromelin, engineer, naval lieutenant, captain and vice admiral.
*Engraving drawn by Danvin and engraved by Dessault from a drawing by J. Milbert, 19th century.*


GREY, Charles, *Pirates of the Eastern Seas*, Sampson Low, Marston & Co, London, 1933.

HEIN, Raymond, *Le Naufrage du* Saint-Géran, Nathan, Paris, 1981.

HERRIEN, Jean-Pierre, *Corsaires!*, Skol Vreiz, Morlaix, 2001.

HÉRUBEL, Michel, *Surcouf, titan des mers*, Perrin, Paris, 1989.

JACQUIN, Philippe, *Sous le pavillon noir*, Gallimard, Paris, 1988.

JOUNOT, Mathilde, *Le Monde de Saint-Malo*, Le Télégramme, St Malo, 1999.

LAGESSE, Marcelle, *Ces hommes de la mer*, Éditions IPC, Mauritius, 1994.

LA HAUSSE DE LALOUVIÈRE, Philippe, *Fortifications côtières*, Éditions P. Lahausse, Mauritius, 1998.

LAILLER, Dan, *Surcouf*, L'Ancre de marine, St Malo, 1995.

LAPOUGE, Gilles, *Pirates, boucaniers, flibustiers*, Éditions du Chêne, Paris, 2002.

LAPOUGE, Gilles, *Les pirates*, Phébus, Paris, 1987.

LA RONCIÈRE, Charles de, *Le flibustier mystérieux*, Éditions Le Masque, Paris, 1934.

LA VARENDE, Jean de, *Surcouf corsaire*, Marcus, Paris, 1946.

LE BRIS, Michel, *L'Épopée de la flibuste (1494–1588)*, Hachette, Paris, 2002.

LE BRIS, Michel and SERNA Virginie, *Pirates, boucaniers et flibustiers des Caraïbes*, Hoë-beke, Paris, 2001.

LENOIR, Philippe, *Île Maurice, ancienne île de France*, Éditions du Cygne, Mauritius, 1979.

LIZÉ, Patrick, *La véritable histoire du pirate Bowen*, Éditions Jacques Glénat, Grenoble, 1987.

MAURICE, Pierre, "L'Île aux trésors", *Islander*, No. 43, Mauritius, April–June 2006.

MERRIEN, Jean, *Histoire des corsaires*, Ancre de marine, Paris, 2003.

MEYER, Jean, *Esclaves et négriers*, Gallimard, Paris, 1986.

NICOLAS, Guy, *Répertoire des capitaines corsaires*, St Malo, 2007.

POIVRE, Pierre, *Mémoires d'un botaniste et explorateur* (revised edition), with commentary by Denis Piat and Jean-Claude Rey, La Découvrance, La Rochelle, 2006.

POIVRE D'ARVOR, Olivier & Patrick, *Chasseurs de trésors*, Place des Victoires, Paris, 2005.

POIVRE D'ARVOR, Olivier & Patrick, *Pirates et corsaires*, Mengès, Paris, 2004.

SURCOUF, Érick, *La Mer en héritage*, Arthaud, Paris, 1992.

SURCOUF, Robert, *Un capitaine corsaire*, Plon, Paris, 1925.

TOUCHARD, Marie-Claude, *L'Aventure du rhum*, Bordas, Paris, 1990.

TOUSSAINT, Auguste, *Avant-Surcouf*, Université de Provence, Aix, 1989.

TOUSSAINT, Auguste, *Histoire de l'océan Indien*, Presses universitaires de France, Paris, 1961.

TOUSSAINT, Auguste, *Les Frères Surcouf*, Flammarion, Paris, 1979.

VAXELAIRE, Daniel, *Les Mutins de la liberté*, Phébus, Paris, 2001.

VAXELAIRE, Daniel, MAURIN, Henri, LENTGE, Jacques, *Mémorial de la Réunion*, Australe Éditions, 1979.

VENTER, Al J., MCKAY, Jeff, and LEVINE, Marie, *Underwater Mauritius*, Ashanti Publishing Limited, Gibraltar, 1989.

WISMES, Armel de, *Pirates et corsaires*, France-Empire, Paris, 1999.